1987

BODY

Keith Campbell was born into an academic family in Wellington, New Zealand, in 1938. He studied at the Victoria University of Wellington and at Oxford in the early 1960s and became a lecturer and then senior lecturer in the University of Melbourne (1963–65). Since 1966 he has worked in the University of Sydney. He was elected to the Australian Academy of the Humanities in 1977 and has been a visiting fellow in the Australian National University and at universities in New Zealand. He is the author of *Metaphysics, An Introduction* (Dickenson, 1976) and of more than thirty contributions to various philosophy journals.

BODY AND MIND

by

KEITH CAMPBELL

Second Edition

UNIVERSITY OF NOTRE DAME PRESS

Notre Dame, Indiana 46556

Second Edition 1984
University of Notre Dame Press edition 1980
First published by Anchor Books, 1970
Reprinted by arrangement with
Doubleday and Company
Copyright © 1970, 1984 by Keith Campbell

Library of Congress Cataloging in Publication Data

Campbell, Keith, 1938–
  Body and mind.

  Bibliography: p.
  Includes index.
  1. Mind and body.   I. Title.
BD450.C244   1984   128'.2   84-13082
ISBN 0-268-00672-5
ISBN 0-268-00673-3 (pbk.)

Manufactured in the United States of America

Contents

PREFACE TO THE SECOND EDITION

This edition differs from the original in including an additional chapter, Chapter 6, *Functionalism,* which sets forth the most important development in the philosophy of mind since this book first appeared in 1970.

The bibliography has been expanded and brought up-to-date with a guide to the literature of Functionalism and with selected additions to the entries concerning other aspects of the Mind-Body problem.

Chapter 1

THE MIND-BODY PROBLEM
AND ITS PLACE IN PHILOSOPHY

(i) What the Problem Is

The problem with which this book deals, the Mind-Body problem, can be posed most briefly in a single question: What is the relation, in a man, between his mind and his body?

The problem is really more general, of course, for if animals other than men, or bodily creatures on other planets, have minds too, then there will be a problem about the relation of their minds to their bodies. I dare say we can generalize whatever conclusion we reach about ourselves to cover animals rather like us, and with luck it might even extend to extraterrestrial beings. In any event men, being concerned most with themselves, have concentrated chiefly on their own case; we will follow this tradition and postpone the wider problem.

So the Mind-Body problem will be for us the problem of determining in what relation a human mind stands to a human body. It is clear that to get a firm grasp of even the problem, let alone its solution, we must also settle two further questions:

What is a human body?
What is a human mind?

The three questions are thoroughly intermingled—a situation quite common in philosophy. Views of what body and mind are help determine answers to the Mind-Body problem, and the troubles involved in some answers to the Mind-Body problem can in turn discredit some opinions about body and mind. Because the questions are so interconnected, when we tackle the Mind-Body problem we must at the same time also work toward answering the questions about mind and body. The Mind-Body problem is three problems rolled into one.

As a first step, we must get clear what we are thinking about in using the terms "body" and "mind".

"Body": Provided you know who *you* are, it is easy to say what your body is: it is what the undertakers bury when they bury you. It is your head, trunk, and limbs. It is the collection of cells consisting of your skin and all the cells inside it. It is the assemblage of flesh, bones, and organs which the anatomist anatomizes. It is the mass of matter whose weight is your weight.

"Mind": What are we talking about when we talk about a man's mind? In philosophy, we need to use words in ways which beg the fewest questions, so a suitably non-committal explanation of the meaning of "mind" begins:

The mind is what differentiates a man from other less interesting objects in the world—plants, rocks, and masses of gas, for example. These other things have no mind. Men are different; "mind" names the difference. But we must be more specific than that. For many features distinguish a man from a rock, a tree, a wax dummy, or a corpse. And most of these differences concern bones, blood, digestion, temperature, skin constitution, and so on, which have nothing in particular to do with the mind. To single out the distinguishing marks of men which are of the "mental" kind, we must confine our attention to differences of activity, not anatomy, between men and mindless beings. Men do all manner of things: jump, laugh, fall, digest, think, build, collide. Of the activities on this short list, a rock can only fall and collide. Trees and corpses are similarly restricted in their range of activity. It is because men do many things that rocks, trees, and corpses do not, that we say they have minds. So more explicitly: To speak of the mind is to speak of the activities which distinguish a man from a rock, tree, dummy, or corpse.

Indeed, so essential is activity to our idea of mind that we sometimes say only beings with minds can *do* anything at all. Things just *happen to* rocks and maybe even trees. On this way of talking, things without minds do not act at all, and have no activities. But whether or not we choose to count colliding, growing, or dying as activities, it is by the range of their activities that beings with minds are distinguished from those without one.

Without begging questions, we can go a bit further and begin an inventory of the mind, a systematic description of the various mental elements. An inventory of the *mental* features of a normal adult includes sensation, perception, thinking, memory, and belief; intention, decision, purpose, action, and want; pain and pleasure, emotion, and mood; and qualities of temperament or personality, such as generosity, courage, or ambition.

We can summarize the inventory by saying that there belong to the mind four overlapping families of items, the families of thinking, acting, feeling, and character. And we can use this summary to state the Mind-Body problem a little more fully. The Mind-Body problem is the problem of what relations hold between the brain and the bag of bones which is your body on the one hand and whatever is involved in the activities of thinking, acting, feeling, and character which distinguish you as a being with a mind on the other. As already noticed, to solve this problem we must at the same time advance fuller accounts of the mind and the body. So far, they have only been pointed out as topics for further investigation.

(ii) Assumptions Involved in the Mind-Body Problem

The Assumption that the Mind Is a Thing

Up to this point we have expressed the Mind-Body problem as a problem concerning the relationship between two things. This is a natural and ordinary way of talking; many expressions in English treat the word "mind" as a noun which, just like "body", denotes a thing. For example: "His mind is clear" ("His body is thin"), "Thoughts raced through his mind" ("Bullets rushed through his body"), "He improved his mind by study," "In senility his mind decayed," and a thousand more.

But it is important to be wary of this assumption, for perhaps the mind is not a thing at all. The incontestable fact that a normal adult *has a mind* (and only one) no more proves that there is such a thing as the mind which he has, than the fact that you *have diabetes* proves that there are such objects as diabetes, some of which you possess, or the fact that someone *gives you the creeps* shows that there are creeps, some of which he hands over.

We must be wary of the assumption because it is exactly what some accounts of the mind—notably, Behavioristic accounts—deny. Behaviorists proceed to a treatment of the Mind-Body problem on the basis that the mind is not a thing. For them, the Mind-Body problem is not a question of the relation of two separate things. It is a question, rather, of how a man's bodily and mental characteristics are related. The Mind-Body problem is, in such cases, perhaps better named the Mental-Physical problem.

Our original way of putting the Mind-Body problem suggests that the mind is a thing. This suggestion is open to challenge, but the challenge affects only the way the Mind-Body problem is posed, and not that problem itself. For we will still want to know in what the mental characteristics of a man consist, and what relation they bear to his physical characteristics. Our problem remains, but it appears in a new light and invites a different solution.

The Assumptions of Homogeneity

Again, the way the Mind-Body problem has been posed so far involves assuming that all of what belongs to the body is of one sort, and all that belongs to the mind is equally of one sort, though perhaps different from the body. We shall later find reason to doubt these assumptions. But they are the correct ones to make initially, for they lead to the simplest accounts of the body and mind. And even if they should be rejected, the Mind-Body problem would remain. What is changed is the expectation that it has a single answer. If mind has no single nature, there will be no single answer to the Mind-Body problem. Instead, the answer will become diverse and complicated.

We have been making a further assumption of homogeneity, i.e., that men are all alike so far as the relation of mind to body is concerned. This is not necessarily so. Maybe the relation of mind to body is different in Tom, Dick, and Harry, or in whites and blacks, or in men and women. In that case a different answer to the Mind-Body problem would be required for each different group involved. But we do not consider such a nightmare until the simpler hypothesis of homogeneity has been discredited, and that has not yet happened.

As before, if these ideas are abandoned, our problem changes but does not disappear. There are, however, other more fundamental assumptions which must be made before any form of the Mind-Body problem arises at all.

The Assumption of Individuality

Whatever we think minds are, the Mind-Body problem presupposes that each normal adult has a mind, has the whole of a mind, has only one mind, and has a mind nobody else has. Maybe this is not the truth. Parmenides and Spinoza both affirmed that all things are one, and our minds, which seem to be distinct, are in reality but aspects of the single divine universe. In Hindu thought the mind's destiny is seen as reunion with the divine mind of which it is a temporarily dislocated part. Jung's notion of a collective unconscious belongs to the same family of ideas which deny that different people, with different bodies, have different and separate minds.

It is clear that without the assumption of individuality our Mind-Body problem quite evaporates. We would have to grapple instead with questions about how the one mind is shared out, and how it is that we know our own thoughts by introspection, but not those of others. There would be many problems. But the question: What is the relation between my body and my mind, and between your body and your mind, which does not hold between my body and your mind? would no longer be a question about any real aspect of our situation. It would just lapse.

The Reality of Matter

We are also taking it for granted that the spatiotemporal world is a reality, a reality independent of us and our knowledge, of which our own body is a part. We take for granted, further, that the spatiotemporal world is material, that is, the concepts of physics and chemistry really apply to it.

Yet one long and respectable tradition in Western thought, that of Idealism, denies this. Bishop Berkeley, for example, held that an apple was a collection of perceptions-as-of-apples whose real existence was as ideas in perceiving minds. In his world there is an infinite idea-generating spirit, God, and finite idea-receiving spirits, you and I, and that is all. There are, in reality, no independent apples, or trees in quads, or independent human bodies. Human bodies are collections of ideas in human minds. And many a philosopher has followed Berkeley in his idealistic doctrine of matter.

If bodies are complex sets of mental items, existing only insofar as they are apprehended, there will be no Mind-Body problem in our sense. Instead, there will be a problem about which sets of ideas constitute bodies, and the Mind-Body problem will become, like the problem of the relation of instincts to minds, a question about the internal economy of the mind.

Equally, if the spatiotemporal world is admitted to be an independent reality, but its material character is denied, the Mind-Body problem undergoes a sea change. This is the course Leibniz took. In his view human bodies were realities independent of any knowledge of them, but they were themselves collections of primitive minds or *monads*. Monads are perceiving and acting things which are not really in space, and so are in no sense material.

If Leibniz is right, the Mind-Body problem becomes a problem concerning the relation between one mind (the one we call our mind) and other minds (which we call our body). So the independent reality of a material world is a precondition for the Mind-Body problem we are discussing.

Challenging and defending each of these assumptions forms in itself a whole branch of philosophy. In this book they must remain as unproven hypotheses under which the whole discussion is conducted. They may not be true, but those of us who think they are can assume them for present purposes with a good conscience.

(iii) The Importance of the Mind-Body Problem

The Mind-Body problem is important in philosophy because of its close connections with philosophy's central concerns. The goal of philosophizing has always been to form the best judgment we can of what man is, what kind of world he inhabits, and what kind of life he should lead. Despite the loss of nerve and gain of modesty characteristic of philosophy in recent times, its problems still concern our place in nature and the lives we should lead. The first of these questions belongs to metaphysics, and the second to ethics, two of the chief departments of philosophy.

Mind's relation to body is involved in our thinking on issues of both metaphysics and ethics. It is clearly at the heart of any view of man's nature. If we hold that our minds are spirits independent of the flesh, or sparks of a divine spirit, or souls reincarnate in the cycle of life, then this must affect profoundly our view of the universe and man's place in it. Our answer to the Mind-Body problem will make all the difference to our beliefs of human origins and human destiny.

As for the problems of ethics, what form of life is best depends on what sort of beings we are. Whether we think of our mind as a free and immortal spirit in temporary bondage to the flesh or contrariwise as bodily in character, mortal, and subject to natural law, will make a vast difference to our view of man's duty, the ends and purposes of life, and the kind of person we should strive to become. The Mind-Body problem, like the problem of God, is thus one of the crucial problems of philosophy; the solution proposed has repercussions through the whole field of our metaphysical and moral opinions.

Study of this problem is important for two further reasons. In thinking about it we continually find ourselves raising other, more abstract and academic philosophical questions. We have already come across an example of this: discussion of the Mind-Body problem should not assume that the mind is a thing. But what does that amount to? What, precisely, must we not assume? To put it rather paradoxically, what is the difference between something which is a thing, and something which is not a thing? When fully worked out, our view of mind and body thus includes an account of what makes a thing a thing—in scholastic jargon, a doctrine of substance. Often as we proceed we will find that the discussion leads off into these more general and more logical problems. Study of the Mind-Body problem can teach us how different issues come to be linked together in philosophy. When we see their connection with the Mind-Body problem we can understand why some men really care about such questions as "What is a cause?" "What is a substance?" "What is a disposition?" which at first sight are academic, dusty, and pathologically irrelevant to human concerns.

The Mind-Body problem also illustrates the relationship between philosophy and other intellectual pursuits, notably in natural science. Philosophy has sometimes fallen into disrepute among sensible men because this relationship has been distorted or misunderstood. The old bad image of philosophy is of an arrogant and foolish armchair dogmatism. Philosophers are seen as proclaiming doctrines as "proven by pure reason" in wanton disregard of what hard experimental and theoretical work might discover. Such a harsh view of philosophy is not dissipated by the spectacle of Aristotle "proving" that the planets move in circles, Descartes rejecting even the possibility of empty space, and Kant arguing that there can be no indeterminacy in physics.

Philosophy's new bad image—miniphilosophy—is one of pedantic triviality. The new distortion affirms that philosophy's concern is solely with bringing to light the content of the concepts men use in their thought about the world. Philosophy is a modest inquiry into the meanings of words and the implications of sentences, and cannot determine truth or falsehood. This view of philosophy as impotent, as no more significant than butterfly collecting, has complex causes in the despair of twentieth-century intellectuals. It was given its most characteristic expression in the thought of Wittgenstein, who said, for example, "Philosophy leaves everything as it is."

I believe both images are caricatures of what philosophy can and should be. Philosophy need neither compete with scientific theory from some allegedly superior vantage point, nor abdicate in favor of some allegedly all-competent and all-conquering science. For all intellectual endeavor, all growth of knowledge, involves both an element of research and an element of reflection. We must both establish facts and weigh their significance, gather data and weld it into a whole view. With the rapid growth of knowledge, a division of intellectual labor has arisen in the West which accords to some men (called "scientists") the task chiefly of establishing particular truths, and to others (called "philosophers") the role of making from those truths, by critical reflection and review, a coherent world vision. People calling themselves scientists often do what is here called philosophy, but what does that matter? There is no antagonism between these pursuits; to judge man and his place in nature we must both find out all we can, and evaluate our findings.

The evaluation leads us into the fields of logic, the analysis of concepts, and studies of the bases of knowledge, all of which are a far cry from observation, experiment, and scientific theorizing. Philosophers specialize on the former tasks, and the differences between these activities and scientific research lead to the caricatures of philosophy. It is true neither that the philosopher in his study can produce unaided a true view of man's nature and prospects, nor that he can do nothing whatever of importance.

We can find the right relations between science and philosophy in attempts to solve the Mind-Body problem. The philosophical inquiry takes its material from the sciences, and so is responsive to change in scientific theory. In taking the widest possible perspective, in scrutinizing all the scientific and common-sense material, the philosopher discharges a necessary task which cannot proceed by direct experimental research.

Science and philosophy are related as ingredients and cake. Ingredients determine what sorts of cake are possible, but they cannot perform their own synthesis. The ingredients change as science changes and we learn more about ourselves, but no scientific theories will alone yield a solution to our general problem about the relations of mind to body in man.

Any solution of the Mind-Body problem will leave hostages to intellectual fortune. It will share the provisional character of all human opinion on substantial general questions. On our view of philosophy, this is as it should be.

Chapter 2

HOW THE MIND-BODY
PROBLEM ARISES

(i) Four Incompatible Propositions

We can grasp what is baffling about the problem of mind and body, and discern a pattern in the rival solutions to it, by setting out four propositions which express in a nutshell the dilemma which confronts us.

(1)   The human body is a material thing.
(2)   The human mind is a spiritual thing.
(3)   Mind and body interact.
(4)   Spirit and matter do not interact.

As was pointed out in Chapter 1, the Mind-Body problem carries with it the problems of what a mind and a body are: propositions (1) and (2) are a most succinct way of giving answers to these questions. Leaving out all detail which for our purposes is irrelevant, they assert an overarching difference of nature between mind and body. This difference sets up the question of how mind and body relate to one another. The details are of no consequence: it does not matter, so far as the Mind-Body problem is concerned, whether the body includes separate digestive and respiratory systems or one organ which handles both tasks. Nor does it matter whether men experience both itches and stings or suffer just one sort of discomfort.

There comes to be a Mind-Body problem when there

comes to be reason for thinking that each of the four propositions is true. For the propositions are incompatible; there is a contradiction involved in asserting all four.

The four propositions form what is known as an *inconsistent tetrad*. That is to say, any three of them are mutually consistent and can all be true. But any three together entail that the fourth is false. It takes at least three of them to disprove the fourth, but any three are enough to dispose of the remaining one.

The incompatibility is strictly logical. From the joint assertion of all four we can derive a contradiction, and not just some proposition known to be false. For example, (1), (2), and (4) entail (5) Mind and body do not interact, and (3) and (5) together are a flat contradiction.

Now the Mind-Body problem is not the problem of finding some profound way to reconcile our four propositions. There is no profound way to reconcile the two sides of a contradiction. Showing how a contradiction can really be true is something that cannot be done. Descartes held that God could do it, but the learned world has not followed him in this. The modern opinion is that there is just no way at all in which the trick can be worked. And wise men will not spend their energies on a task not even God can perform. They will not attempt the impossible task of reconciling the four propositions.

Rather, the Mind-Body problem consists in determining which of the four propositions is false. A satisfactory solution of the problem consists in identifying the false propositions (for there may be more than one), explaining how, despite their plausibility, they are nevertheless false, and filling out as far as possible the details of the true propositions which remain.

In this chapter we explain more fully what the four propositions mean, and consider the reasons there are for thinking that each of them is true. For each of them does have a good deal of initial plausibility. If that were not so, there would be no Mind-Body problem. An inconsistent tetrad cannot by itself make a problem of anything, for if one of its members is clearly false, we reject it and our difficulties evaporate.

We explain the four propositions by discussing the technical terms involved.

"Material"

In calling the body "material" I mean that it shares the properties common to the most familiar objects of our environment, such as shoes, ships, and lumps of sealing wax, e.g., mass, position, volume, velocity; that it is composed entirely of the recognized material stuffs, e.g., carbon, nitrogen, oxygen, phosphorus; and that its responses to physical influences satisfy only the laws governing all matter, whether found in living organisms or in inanimate systems. Proposition (1), asserting the material nature of the body, thus asserts that physiology is just a specially complicated branch of chemistry and physics—and chemistry in its turn reduces to physics.

Now physics changes from one year to the next, with the result that the sorts of events which conform to physical laws can change from one year to the next. What the claim to materiality amounts to changes as physics changes. In the eighteenth century, (1) would assert that all events involving the body can be explained by reference solely to impact and gravitation among particles. And this is false, for the body is electromagnetic as well as mechanical. In the twentieth century, (1) embraces electromagnetism, for that is part of contemporary physics. The content of the claim that an object is material is relative to the physics of the time it is made. This *relativity of materialism* is of great importance when we come to consider materialist doctrines of the mind. The claim that, for example, the mind is the same thing as the (purely material) central nervous system, inherits the relativity of all materialism.

There is another complication about materiality. A material thing need not always behave in accord with physical law. A stone which flies through the air under a miraculous divine propulsion would violate the dynamical laws governing the motion of stones. But it would remain a material thing for all that. A material thing can, without ceasing to be a material thing, respond to forces other than physical ones. The brain, without ceasing to be material, can act under the influence of an immaterial mind. What is necessary is that all *physical* forces acting on the object should always have their normal effect even if this is supplemented, from time to time, by supervening influences.

Now suppose an object—a brain, let us say—in which events of a physical kind occur. Some of these events are determined, and are subject to physical law. But others do not conform to physical law; they lie even beyond the latitude allowed in quantum physics. If these irregular events are the outcome of divine or spiritual action, the situation is the same as that for the stone. If, however, the irregular events are *undetermined*, and conform to no law, physical or superphysical, we cannot think of them as arising from the operation of a non-physical force. For where there is a force there is a law by which it operates. A brain in which there are undetermined irregular physical events is a brain which, although acted on only by physical influences, is not at every point subject to the laws governing material things. It would not be a *purely material object*.

If in a brain there are events which are not of a physical kind, then whether they are law-conforming or random, the brain in which they occur is not a purely material object. In saying that a body is purely material, we are committed to holding that only events of a physical kind occur within it, and that either there are no deviations from physical expectations beyond the limits allowed in quantum theory, or that influences other than physical ones are effective in it.

There is one more point to notice. If events other than physical ones occur in an object, then that object is not purely material. But if these non-physical events make no difference to what happens, if they are idle, then so far as physical events and qualities are concerned, the object can conform entirely to physical law. There need be no departures from physical expectation whatever. It is only if the non-physical events are idle that this can happen; if they are not idle, there must be a departure from physical law. Such a situation, with idle non-physical characteristics, is important for Epiphenomenalist theories of mind discussed toward the end of the book. In such a case, it seems to me better to describe the object as "material plus", rather than "not material", which suggests behavior incompatible with the physical determination of events.

"Spiritual"

Saying what is meant by proposition (2), that the human mind is a spiritual thing, is no easy task. The spiritual is so elusive that it seems to evade definition no less than investigation. The mind seems to have, *as mind*, no special nature at all. It resists direct description. So we begin to specify the spiritual by contrasting it with matter. A spiritual object is one which does not have all the qualities of matter; it lacks at least some of: mass, volume, velocity, solidity. Many thinkers have defined the spiritual, in contrast to matter, as being completely non-spatial and hence as having *none* of matter's characteristic qualities. But if ghosts are any guide, it seems that mass and solidity are the ones that count, for ghosts would have position and shape.

Further, a spiritual thing is *not* composed of the ordinary material elements, and *not* subject to ordinary material laws. We need to proceed a little carefully here. A shaft of light is not composed of ordinary material elements. Nor is it solid. In both these ways it resembles a ghost. But its behavior does conform to physical laws and the particles which make it up play a part in the economy of the non-thinking, non-living, spatiotemporal world. A shaft of light is therefore not spiritual. Likewise a magnetic field, even if it is a thing, is not spiritual. Though a magnetic field lacks most qualities of material things, it belongs to the inanimate space-time world. And any part of the inanimate space-time world is excluded from the realm of spirit.

All this is negative. Just what features a spirit *does* have are still to be specified. We must give the spirit some positive qualities, else it will not be anything at all. For what does not exist is without material qualities, is not composed of material elements, is not subject to physical laws, and is no part of inanimate nature.

The choice of a positive defining characteristic for spirit must be made with some care. To preserve the contrast with matter, we will do best to pick a characteristic which material things do not have. And to give the term "spirit" a useful role in our thought, we will do best to pick a characteristic which men's minds do have, or at least seem to. And so as not to exclude partially developed or handicapped spirits by our definition, we must choose a characteristic broad enough in scope to embrace all the sorts of spirit we might wish to talk about. There are two characteristics which have appealed to philosophers as meeting these specifications: consciousness and intentionality.

Consciousness

Descartes defined the spiritual thing which is a man's mind as *res cogitans,* the thinking thing. By this he meant the thing which enters any conscious state, whether of thinking, feeling, or acting.

The problem for this definition was deep and dreamless sleep. If in sleep there is no consciousness then equally, by definition, there is no spirit. A man would have to be given a new spirit, and so be a different man, every time he woke up. Descartes, a bold and brave philosopher, confronted this problem squarely and affirmed that the mind is conscious at all times, even in sleep. We don't realize this, he believed, because we forget the greater part of our dreams.

It is true that we forget much of our dreaming. But there is no reason to think that at every moment of sleep, trance, or anesthesia, there is some conscious mental activity. The mind is active, perhaps, but not conscious. So the nearest we should go to Descartes' definition of spiritual substance is: a spiritual substance must be *capable* of consciousness. The spirit is something which can think, feel, and act. The intrinsic character of this thing capable of conscious thought, feeling, and action—what it's like when it's resting, so to speak—remains unspecified.

So the whole account of spirit remains rather shadowy. A spirit is defined indirectly as something capable of consciousness, and consciousness is no more fully described than as "what it takes to think, feel, and act," that is, as what it takes to have a mind.

Intentionality

"Intentionality" is a technical notion. It is used to describe a peculiar and significant characteristic of mental states. A hope is not just a hope, it is a hope for something, more or less definite. I can hope to obtain the moon, or win the girl, or get to work on time. I cannot just hope. Despair is despair over something. I can despair over my son's addiction to drugs or my being shipwrecked and not rescued. I cannot just despair. Perception is perception of something; I don't just see, I see an object or event or circumstance. I see the car, or I see the car crashing, or I see that the car has crashed. When I think, I think about the problem in hand. Anger is anger at someone or something. Determination is determination to achieve something.

Other terms, which have no connection with the mind, are like this too. A substance can't just be poisonous, it must be a poison for some sorts of creatures. I can't just collide, I must collide with something. But the peculiarity of the mental states is that they are directed on objects which need have no material existence. I cannot collide with a boat unless there is a boat to collide with. But I can be determined to rescue the drowning passengers even if there are no passengers. Being directed on objects which need have no material existence is what is significant when mental states are described as intentional.

A mental state is determined by its intentional object; my hope is the hope it is, and not some other, because it has one intentional object and not some other. And these intentional objects need not, in any material sense, exist at all.

Intentionality is thus a likely candidate for defining the spiritual. It seems to maintain the contrast of the spiritual with the material, for material descriptions are not intentional. And it seems also to give "spiritual" a real place in our thought, for it is the familiar capacities to think, decide, and hope, etc., which are described in intentional ways. This is much more promising than a definition in terms of absolutely Free Will or survival of bodily death, which maintain the distinction of matter from spirit, but rest upon quite dubious human capacities. We might therefore try to define a spiritual thing as something which has intentional states.

There are nonetheless difficulties with this definition. Maybe not all mental states have intentionality. States of bodily feeling are one doubtful class. To itch is to be in a mental state. An itch in the small of my back has a location, but it does not seem to have an object in the way that a hope does. Moods are another doubtful class. Dread, depression, and light-heartedness seem to need no objects, although we might try to overcome this objection either by saying they have extremely general objects, such as the state of the world, or my condition and prospects, or by holding that they involve other mental states, such as intending to climb the flagpole, which might have ordinary intentional objects.

The claim that *all* mental states are intentional may be true, but it will take some hard work to prove it. The Mind-Body problem will require of us, sooner or later, a complete philosophy of the mind, in which the whole range of mental conditions is properly classified and analyzed.

If not all mental states are intentional, a definition of spirit in terms of intentionality will lead to the conclusion that some facets of the mind are spiritual, while others are not. This may well be the correct view, but it is not good to divide the mind in this way right from the beginning. A definition of spirit should leave open the possibility that even though their descriptions in ordinary language differ, states of mind are all of the same nature.

Another difficulty is that some material things may be describable in intentional terms. An intentional description differs from a material one and yet a material thing may have states which are intentionally described. Thus a computer may be calculating the square root of 493; "calculating the square root of 493" is an intentional description. The calculation is directed upon its solution and is identified by reference to it. And if the computer is calculating the integral square root of 493, it is directed upon a non-existent object. Yet the computer is a material thing. So even if our definition of spirit does refer to intentionality, it will have to include the negative reference to immateriality as well.

Attempts to supply the positive element in the definition of "spirit" using consciousness and intentionality tend to coincide. For the one leads to "something which is capable of thinking, feeling, and acting," while the other leads to "something with intentionally describable states," where thinking, feeling, and acting are exactly the activities to which intentional descriptions apply.

Both give us indirect descriptions in terms of capacities, and both require the negative supplement to keep matter and spirit distinct. We can sum them up thus:

"Spiritual" = "immaterial, and capable of mental life."

The idea of spirituality proves to add only immateriality to the idea of mentality. Proposition (2), which asserts the spirituality of the mind amounts to:

The mind is an immaterial thing capable of mental life.

The search for a direct positive definition of "spirit" which would enlarge our knowledge of non-material reality is thus a failure. So even if we decide, in the end, that the mind is a spiritual thing, we will remain in considerable ignorance.

The spirit eludes positive description except in terms

of its capabilities. But does this really make it any different from matter? In pursuing the Mind-Body problem, we stumble here upon one of the most profound problems in metaphysics and the philosophy of science, i.e., the problem of the extent to which physical descriptions are descriptions of capacities possessed by objects whose inner reality remains unspecified.

"Interaction"

In our four propositions, the only other technical term is "interact". It is quickly explained: two items interact if and only if each has an effect upon the other. In action, changes in one item cause changes in another. In interaction, the process is mutual. The interaction which particularly concerns us involves bodily causes of mental effects and mental causes of bodily effects.

(ii) The Initial Plausibility of All Four Propositions

We said earlier that there is a Mind-Body problem only because there is some reason to think that each one of the four members of our inconsistent tetrad is true. It is time to substantiate this claim by reviewing the case which can be made for each of the propositions considered independently.

1. The Body Is a Material Thing

This proposition asserts that the body is composed of ordinary matter. It is made up of atoms of familiar elements—carbon, oxygen, nitrogen, and so on. And those atoms are in turn composed of the same particles which make up such atoms wherever they are found. The proposition asserts further that the material making up the body, provided only physical forces are acting on it, obeys all and only the very physical laws of motion, combination, and dissolution which hold for inanimate matter.

The grounds for 1. are scientific. The findings of chemistry and biochemistry all point in this direction. Now that chemistry has developed to the point where we can determine the elementary constitution of material things, we can affirm with confidence that the vital functions—for example, respiration, digestion, and temperature-conservation—involve no transmutation of elements into some new kind of living stuff. Now that biochemistry has made the stunning advances of recent years, we know that these processes proceed in accord with the very laws governing the behavior of matter in an inanimate environment. The unraveling of the DNA maze has enabled us to discover that even growth, replication, and the transmission of hereditary characteristics are processes of an ordinary chemical kind. The molecules involved are more complex, but the atoms gain no new nature in the living organism.

It is hard to appreciate how radically the outlook on living bodies has changed in modern times. To learn that in all the variety of inanimate nature there are but one hundred different kinds of atom is surprise enough. To be assured that in addition all living things, at first sight so radically different, make use of just part of the same basic atomic inventory would be incredible if the evidence were not unchallengeable.

Wherever we have been able to isolate an organic

process and judge with confidence just which physical forces are at work, we have found that the living matter's behavior has conformed with ordinary physics and ordinary chemistry. The human body, including its brain, is not different in constitution or atomic nature from its material environment. That is proposition 1., and its warrant is the success of the biochemistry and biophysics which affirm it.

Yet although a body is a material system, a man may not be. To settle the Mind-Body problem we must determine whether this material bodily system is sometimes or always subject to further, non-physical forces and influences, and if so, which ones.

2. The Mind Is a Spiritual Thing

That the mind thinks and feels, and that it is engaged in action, are not contentious propositions. They help to pick out what we are talking about when we talk about minds. There can be little more argument over them than over claims that dentists drill teeth and politicians are engaged in the affairs of state. At worst such propositions may fall into disrepute like the claim that witches cast spells, which became discredited when we discovered that there is only appearance and no reality in the operation of casting spells. But thinking, feeling, and deciding are so much a part of our self-knowledge that we can neglect the idea that there is no reality in them.

So the crucial element of proposition 2. is the immateriality of the mind. There are four families of reasons upon which men have based their conviction that the mind is not material.

Traditional and Intuitive Grounds

The differences between men on the one hand and our inanimate environment on the other are so many and so striking that the materiality of the mind has seemed to most people an obvious impossibility. Men can see and hear, ponder and resolve, suffer and enjoy. They have a language and a culture. They can make plans, solve problems, and hunger and thirst after righteousness. They can anticipate and regret, hope and fear. They can love, they can be amused, they can make music, they can worship. They can be heroic or cruel or ambitious. In all of this they are utterly different from the rocks and puddles, furniture and utensils, and even plants and animals which make up our natural and artificial environment. Further, these differences are all ones in which mind plays a crucial part. It is clear that men have got something that floorboards lack; "mind" is the name of this extra possession. But floorboards are not deficient in materiality. They are fully and properly material things. What is more natural, then, but to conclude that the mind is not material? So has arisen the long Western tradition of contrasting man with the natural material realm. For Plato man comes into it as a prisoner, for Christians he journeys through it as a wayfarer, for contemporary Existentialists he finds himself thrown amid alien *things.*

Recall the old bad words we have for matter: matter is brute, inert, blind, senseless, and purposeless. Mind on the other hand is light, subtle, discerning. Matter is stodgy; minds see visions and dream dreams. Matter is passive; minds create, act, and strive. Our entire religious tradition with its huge impact on how men see themselves has made the spiritual character of the mind seem the plainest of truths.

Now this tradition of immaterialism, based as it is on a common sense which incorporates massive ignorance of the ways of the world, cannot by itself establish anything. Its importance is rather that of placing the responsibility of proof on him who denies the spiritual character of the mind. The structure of the argument is this:

There are great differences between men and other material things.

These differences require an explanation.

The initially most plausible explanation is that men differ from material things in having a spirit responsible for what is distinctively human.

So he who denies the spirituality of the mind must show how something merely material can after all have all the human characteristics.

This first body of reasons, then, are more accurately described as reasons for believing the mind is spiritual in the absence of convincing proof to the contrary. We are here discussing initial plausibility; the initially plausible view of the mind is that it is spiritual, because the mind is responsible for such an astonishing range of phenomena. Attempts at passing beyond initial plausibility to positive demonstration that the mind is not material have taken three main forms:

Epistemic Grounds

We can come to know for ourselves, and not just by teaching or report, only if the thing known affects our minds. Now we can learn of the world in ways other than by the physical operation of the senses. The mind is affected by non-physical reality.

For example, mathematical knowledge is not sense knowledge. The eternal, immaterial numbers are not perceptible, yet we can know them. Numbers cannot have any effect upon matter, yet they can affect our minds. So minds cannot be material.

Likewise men can, in this life by mystic union and in the life to come by beatific vision, come to a knowledge of God. But God is not perceptible. We do not come to know him by any transaction involving the senses.

Again, we can know non-physical aspects of material things. Men have the knowledge of good and evil. But the good and evil in things cannot be seen or felt. We come to the knowledge of values through the operation of a "higher" spiritual faculty.

So, the argument runs, in at least these three cases the mind is open to influences which cannot affect matter. In consequence, the mind cannot be a purely material thing. Again, if the changes which consist in gaining knowledge of these kinds are not bodily changes, then the mind is a spiritual thing.

Logical Grounds

Many arguments have been developed attempting to show that the idea that the mind is material is logically impossible or incoherent. These arguments fall into two distinct classes: Category Arguments and Mental-Object Arguments. Here is an example of each.

Category Arguments

Consider pains. The favorite materialist idea about pains is that they are states of the brain. Now a pain can be intense or weak, long-lived or short, continuous or intermittent, stinging or throbbing. But there is no sense at all in saying a pain is two inches long, or of high voltage, or has electric currents in it that are fast or slow. So the idea that a man can have a small, cubical, low voltage, circular current pain makes no more sense than the idea that a dog can have an odd, prime, factor-of-25 doghouse. Just as a doghouse is not the sort of thing that can be odd or prime or have any arithmetical property, so a pain is not the sort of thing which can have any physical property of the kind a brain-state has. Doghouses and numbers, pains and brain-states, come from different *categories.* To confuse categories is to talk nonsense; and nonsense cannot be true. We reach the same result whatever material item we choose to equate with a pain. And what holds for pains holds for anything mental. So the mind cannot be material.

Mental-Object Arguments

Take an afterimage. An afterimage is not nothing. There is a difference between someone who is having an afterimage and someone who is not. Suppose the afterimage is pale turquoise. Now it may be that nothing nearby, either inside or outside the head of the person having the afterimage, is pale turquoise. If there does happen to be something pale turquoise nearby, it is almost certainly not the afterimage. The afterimage is "in the mind," but it is not a material thing. So the mind in which it is, is not a material thing either.

Anyone who proposes to defend the material nature of the mind must show how to rebut the category and mental-object arguments, for otherwise they refute his position.

Empirical Grounds

Scientific investigation points to the materiality of the body. We must now ask whether any comparable body of research establishes the nature of the mind. The situation is a curious one. We might expect that just as biochemistry and biophysics yield a result for the body, so psychology would settle the question for the mind. But this is not so.

Psychological research has established, with hitherto unknown precision, many of the relationships between mental events and processes, for example, between expectation and perception. And it has explored relations between mental and physical events and processes, for example, in experiments concerning the threshold levels for perception. Psychologists develop theories of personality structure and motivation. They increase our knowledge of how people learn and how they cope with distress.

But psychological investigation does not yield a doctrine of the nature of the mind. Psychological technique does not determine whether or not the mind is material. The chief reason for this is that psychologists must operate principally with the data of stimulus and response, and these data do not specify the nature of the mind falling between them. The Behaviorism which identifies the mind with behavior patterns displayed by human organisms has been very influential in psychology, and Behaviorism is indeed a doctrine of the mind's nature. But Behaviorism is a philosophical thesis and not just a result of scientific psychological investigation.

The empirical evidence urged for the spirituality of the mind is rather that of parapsychology, the unorthodox investigation of extraordinary capacities of mind. This evidence is of two types: that concerning paranormal psychological powers, such as telepathy and clairvoyance, and that concerning survival of death. Telepathy and clairvoyance involve gaining knowledge of the thoughts of another, or of matter of physical fact, without the use of normal sensory means. The evidence of survival is that involved in "communications" to a trance-medium of knowledge hitherto possessed only by a now deceased person.

If any of these phenomena are genuine, they establish that the mind is not merely material. They show that a mind can do what no material system can do. Remembering the relativity of materialism, we may hope that a new physics and chemistry will be able to accommodate them. But until that happens, or computers start to display inexplicable paranormal powers, paranormal phenomena would provide the best of reasons for holding to the spiritual character of the mind.

Although the prima facie case for the mind's spirituality does not rest on a copious base of relevant scientific results, it is nevertheless many-sided and considerable. Of our four incompatible propositions, the first two together set up a duality in man's nature. This duality of matter and spirit generates the problems of interaction between them which give to the Mind-Body conundrum its modern severity.

3. Mind and Body Interact

This proposition is one of those, supported by an enormous and ever growing mass of common experience, which form a starting point for investigation and speculation. We confirm the interaction of mind and body a hundred times a day. A hot stove burns my finger (bodily event), and in consequence I suffer pain (mental event). I take LSD (bodily event), and am afflicted with hallucinations (mental event). The stray light entering my eyes changes in composition, and I realize that the traffic light has changed to green. So bodily changes have mental effects.

Causal connections in the other direction, linking mind to body, are equally easy to find. I am suffering the pain of my burned finger (mental event), and this causes me to apply a burn cream (bodily event). My psychedelic hallucinations are terrifying, so I scream or go to the hospital. I realize the traffic lights have changed, so I accelerate.

We can bolster the case for mind-body interaction by more general considerations. If the pain in the example of the burn is not caused by the physical contact of flesh with hot stove, then either it has no cause at all, or it has some utterly mysterious and totally unconscious prior mental cause. Neither alternative has any great theoretical appeal. We might come to one of these positions as a last resort when all alternatives have been ruled out, but they have low rational priority.

Again, in considering the action of mind on body, we might eventually come to the conclusion that mental events of thinking and planning formed no part of the causal chain resulting in the appearance of Newton's *Principia* or the Concorde airliner. But we should arrive at this complicated and implausible position reluctantly, and only after fruitless exploration of every other avenue.

The claim that mind and body interact, well-confirmed though it be, may not be true. We may even come in the end to reject it. But if we deny mind-body interaction we must furnish a convincing account of how the illusion arises. We will need a powerful reinterpretation of all the evidence apparently supporting interaction. In the meantime, the initial plausibility of the view that both body acts on mind and mind acts on body is immense.

4. Spirit and Matter Do Not Interact

The Mind-Body problem, what Schopenhauer called the "world-knot", is complete when we see that there are good reasons for *denying* that matter and spirit can interact. The case for this is a dual one; it rests on theoretical considerations and on a concrete program of scientific research.

Theoretical Considerations

The theoretical consideration is simply stated: interaction of matter and spirit is a causal impossibility. To see the force of this idea, we must make some study of the philosophy of cause. In a causal sequence, there is at least an event c followed by another event e. If what is involved is a single causal link and not a whole chain, the events c and e must not be too remote from one another in space (some say they must be next to each other), nor too far separated in time (again, some say c and e must be simultaneous or immediately successive). To distinguish cause from mere coincidence the whole class C of events relevantly similar to c must be followed by events of class E, relevantly similar to e. (Pretend, for our purposes, that you know what "relevantly similar" means.)

The Pure Regularity Theory of Causes, which springs from the thought of David Hume, holds the causal relation between c and e to consist in no more than the existence of the class C-E of sequences of which c-e is an example. The Pure Regularity Theory identifies causal connection with regularity of sequence. Since no limits can be placed on what sort of event can be in regular connection with what other sort of event, there can, on this theory, be causal connections between any two events, no matter how diverse. No sort of connection can be a causal impossibility. Anything can be the cause of anything. In particular, provided that problems about their spatial relations can be ironed out, material events can be the cause of spiritual events and vice versa.

Proposition 4. asserts that matter and spirit do not interact. Its theoretical support collapses entirely if the Pure Regularity Theory of cause is correct. To maintain the theoretical objection to interaction, the Pure Regularity Theory must be convicted of error. Here, as so often, the Mind-Body problem raises one of the crucial general questions of philosophy. This time it is the problem: What is a cause?

Let us consider, in brief compass, the objections to the Pure Regularity Theory on which the theoretical case against the interaction of matter with spirit relies.

In developed sciences, we do not rest content with the mere establishment of a regular succession among events, but seek to uncover the mechanisms, the mode of operation, whereby the cause-event issues in the effect-event. It is not enough to know that assembling a critical mass of radioactive uranium will give you an explosion; we want to know why this happens. The story of why this happens is an explanation connecting the nature of uranium with a series of processes which culminate in an explosion. This intervening series of processes is what, with a slight stretching of the word, we are calling the "mechanism" of the causal connection.

Connections which are not fundamental thus do not fit the Pure Regularity Theory, for they involve reference to a mechanism as well as to regular sequence. When our analysis comes to an end in "fundamental" connections, for example, an atomic nucleus absorbing a flying particle and then dividing, there are no intervening processes between cause and effect (or none we know about, anyway). That is what we mean when we call the connection fundamental. We cannot say how or why a fundamental process occurs. In these cases we must rest content with equations giving accurate quantitative expression to what happens, where, and when. In the atomic absorption and division example, we specify what energies are released, in what direction, over what time. In this case too the Pure Regularity

Theory does not cover the whole of what is required; it leaves out the requirement that the regularity must be given mathematical form.

Now all causal ties either have a mechanism, or are fundamental and admit of mathematical expression. But the links between matter and spirit neither have a mechanism nor admit of mathematical expression. The reason lies in the impalpable character of spirit. We have no idea how a mechanism could "get a grip" on a spirit. The mechanism by which changes in the brain can "get a grip" on the heart and change its rate of beating is intelligible; but how could the brain get a grip on a spiritual mind, to give it fear? And further, because fear resists description in terms of place or direction, we have no "fear" equations linking brain and spirit, nor seem likely ever to have any. From which the conclusion drawn is: matter-spirit interaction is impossible.

These theoretical considerations are not absolutely compelling. They establish at most the *anomaly* of matter-spirit interaction. They show that any such interactions would be very different from the interactions characteristic of physical sciences, and very difficult to express properly. These strange connections would exist only in the fragment of the universe consisting of beings with minds. "Nomological danglers" is the abusive term Feigl introduced to describe such anomalous relations. Of course calling a fact anomalous will not make it go away. Of course, if spirit is a rare and peculiar stuff any causal relations it has to matter will be rare and different from those characteristic of the physical sciences.

The importance of the theoretical considerations is

in showing matter-spirit interactions to be mysterious oddities quite at variance with what we know of nature's workings. "Don't dabble in mysterious oddities any more than you must" is a sound principle of intellectual method. On this principle matter-spirit interaction must be accorded low rational priority. We must seek ways of avoiding the admission of such an idea to our theories.

Empirical Considerations

Even if we are prepared to countenance the possibility of matter-spirit interaction, there are investigations which point to the conclusion that there are in fact no such connections. We shall call this scientific evidence The Shadow of Physiology.

Brain activity is the crucial bodily factor in both learning of our environment (perception), and in living out our lives in that environment (action). The links of senses to brain, and brain to muscles show every sign of being physicochemical relations. So if spirit acts on matter in men, it acts through the brain. Yet the evidence suggests that nothing happens in a man save what conforms to physical and chemical law.

The ancients believed that plants and animals enjoyed the same material constitution as inanimate things, but obeyed different laws, controlled by vegetative and animal souls. For intelligent men without the benefit of neurophysiological research this was a very sensible belief. For animals, scientific advances have not yet conclusively exploded it. Our ignorance of brains is still profound, but research based on the assumption that the brain obeys only physicochemical laws has not yet suffered a damaging reverse. There seems to be no room for spirit to get into the act, and no sign of its effects. The Shadow of Physiology is a shadow cast by a successful program of scientific research.

The importance of this speculative extension of physiology for the Mind-Body problem is plain, for it is incompatible with matter-spirit interaction. How different our view of man would be if brain physiology uncovered the operation of non-physical forces! In tackling the Mind-Body problem we must come to terms with the scientific results and the likelihoods these results reveal. They reveal that the outlook for the action of spirit on matter in particular, and so for interaction, is bleak.

The Mind-Body problem is a problem because, as we have now seen, there are reasons for holding to each of the four propositions which make up our inconsistent tetrad. Competing solutions of the problem consist in competing ideas concerning which members of the tetrad should be rejected, and what should be put in their place. So now we must set out and assess these different responses that the tetrad has called forth.

Chapter 3

DUALISMS

Dualist doctrines are those which, in holding that the body is material and the mind spiritual, accord to man a dual nature. Dualists retain the first two of our four propositions, and must therefore reject either the third or fourth. So there are two main types of Dualism, one affirming and the other denying the interaction of mind and body.

Before discussing each of these alternatives, we must consider general objections to the very idea of a spiritual thing, for if these objections were compelling they would of course rule out both types of Dualism. Some of these objections are purely philosophical, and some are more closely tied to scientific findings.

(i) Philosophical Objections to Spirit

If spirits were spatial, then we would have to show why they were not just a new variety of physical thing, like a magnetic field. And we would have to face the idea that two different things can be in the same place at the same time. These problems are not overwhelming; we can distinguish spirits from material objects by reference to mental properties, and we can point out that, like an electrostatic field and a piece of glass, two different things can be in the same space provided they are of suitably different kinds. So a body and a spirit might well coexist in the same space.

Spatial spirits would nevertheless give us many intractable problems. How could we determine the boundaries of spiritual things? What is the composition of such ghosts? What holds them together? What makes them move? The worry that these questions could never be answered has led philosophers to hold that spirits have no spatial characteristics at all, not even position. But there is usually a price to be paid for avoiding one set of problems. Theories dealing in things which have no place are heir to several ills of their own.

The Elusiveness of Spirit

Being without place, a spirit resists normal research techniques. If we want to investigate such a thing, we literally do not know where to begin. We cannot devise experiments in which spiritual operations are controlled, or screened, or maximized. In attempts to enlarge our knowledge of spirits, we are restricted to introspection and asking other people, whose bodies we suppose are also connected with a spirit. By the experimental use of drugs or hypnotism, for example, we might hope to gain more copious and accurate insight into spirit's nature and workings, but we are always confined to reports on how things seem to the subject of research. Uncontrolled reports of how things seem are an unsatisfactory basis for scientific knowledge. A theory which involves spirits is therefore one which, of necessity, involves a great deal of ignorance. Spirits are methodologically elusive.

Like so many other considerations in the philosophy of mind, the methodological elusiveness of spirits will not of course establish that there are no such objects. But it should set us to searching for adequate alternative accounts of the mind which are less impervious to scientific investigation.

The Correlation of Minds and Bodies

A fact about normal people, so familiar we scarcely notice it, is that each body has associated with it one, and only one, mind. And with each different body is associated a different mind. Each mind belongs with the body through which it perceives and acts, and with no other. The bodies and minds of people match one to one.

In all Dualist theories, this is a contingent and indeed surprising fact about the world. It is a fact that cries out for explanation. The explanation is not going to be easy to find if the spirit is not only distinct from the body but is not in space at all. How can a non-spatial thing enter exclusive and intimate relations with just one body and no other? Take the case of two bodies which are thoroughly alike; identical twins just before birth. Suppose that from the time of the first division their development has proceeded exactly parallel. They now differ only in position and physical attitude, so their only differences are spatial. Yet already (or soon after) each body must be associated with its own mind. If these minds are non-spatial spirits, how can they "take advantage" of the merely spatial differences between the twins' bodies and become associated with just one of them? It will be hard for any Dualist to furnish a convincing account of such a situation.

The Individuation of Spirits

Non-spatial spirits are involved in another, deeper, conundrum. Minds can be more or less like one another. Two people can be very different indeed, or they can be broadly alike in upbringing, education, experience, taste, and character. Suppose that they are not just very alike, but absolutely alike. By some freak of nature, the course of their experience has been exactly alike and has worked in exactly the same way on the same innate tendencies. The minds of these two persons are alike in both history and contents.

On the Dualist theory each has a spirit just like the other's. But here an embarrassment arises: In what sense are there *two* spirits? What is the difference between *two* spirits each with the same contents and history as the other, and *one* spirit associated with two bodies? This is not the question of how we could tell that there were two minds, or how we could tell which was which. In a spontaneous fission explosion of radioactive uranium, we may not be able to tell which atom disintegrated first or whether the chain reaction began from a single atom or from two disintegrating simultaneously. Nevertheless, although we may not have them, there are answers to the questions "Which atom?" and "One atom or two?" The answers involve the location of the atoms in question at the time the reaction began. The atom which initiated the reaction was the atom at the place where the chain commenced at the time it commenced. If atoms at different places disintegrate, then two atoms are involved. Atoms, and material things generally, are individuated and counted by their positions. Non-spatial spirits cannot, of course, be individuated and counted in this way. But then, in what way can they be individuated and counted? If there really is no difference between one spirit and two spirits of exactly similar history and contents, then spirits are a very suspect sort of thing indeed.

Spirits as Located

As Locke realized, Dualists have made things unnecessarily hard. Spirits can be given a location even if they have no dimensions. They need not take up space in any direction, so need have no length, area, or volume. Yet if they are at a place, and in particular at a place inside a body, progress can be made with the problems of correlation and individuation that have just been raised. Spirits are correlated with the body within which they lie. As bodies exclude one another, there will be exactly one body containing, and so associated with, each spirit. A place inside the skull is a sensible location for the spirit, and skulls interpenetrate to a negligible extent. So no spirit will be in more than one body. Why only one spirit is to be found inside a normal man is not answered in this way, nor how the body and spirit interact. But there is some intelligibility in the notion that a body can affect and be affected by a spirit within it and not by any spirit beyond it. An indwelling spirit does have a special relation to one body rather than others, no matter how similar these other bodies might be.

Further, indwelling spirits can be individuated by the bodies within which they are located. The bodies can be individuated spatially, no matter how alike they may be in every other way, and the indwelling spirits can be individuated in the same way. If they are in different places at one time, there are two of them; if not, there is only one. We would not know precisely at which point the spirit was located, but that is not a problem. The problem of individuation is "In what do two spirits differ, in virtue of which there are two and not one?" And we can answer "They are two in virtue of different location" even if we do not know what their exact location is.

If we give spirits a location we are also able to meet the more subtle and more difficult objections raised by P. F. Strawson against the possibility of a pure ego —what we are calling a "spirit". And for the same reason, that location enables spirits to be identified and distinguished from one another.[1]

Strawson's conclusion, that anything to which we ascribe a conscious state must also have bodily characteristics, and so cannot be a separate object "attached" to the body, is seen to be too strong when we notice that a located spirit, "attached" to the body, will meet his objections about the identity of spirits.

What could be more natural than the idea that when you go on holiday you take your mind with you? And if your mind is a spirit, how explain this unless the spirit is to be found where your body is?

Descartes, the great Dualist who set the modern debate in motion, conceded that the non-spatial spirit

---

[1] See P. F. Strawson, *Individuals* (London, 1959), chap. 3, especially pp. 90–103. Strawson's further objection to spirits, that there could never be adequate grounds for describing them in mental or any other terms, involves a positivistic view of imperceptible objects discussed in chapters 4 and 5 below.

worked through a particular place in the body.[2] (He bet wrong, putting his money on the pineal gland rather than the cortex, but that's of no importance.) Here we propose to take the matter one step further and allow that the spirit is actually at a particular place.

The minimum spatiality that this requires is location; dimension need not come into it. The great modern neurophysiologist Sir John Eccles, who is a Dualist, accords "spatial patterning" to the mind.[3] This goes further than what is needed for individuation and intimacy of association, and it raises problems of its own about size, shape, and volume which do not trouble a theory of merely located spirit.

In the eighteenth century the natural philosopher Boscovich developed a theory of matter in which the fundamental elements were material points. Any doctrine of located spirits involves spiritual points, and these would have to be distinguished from material points. So far as spatial properties are concerned, they are of course indistinguishable. It is in terms of what is to be found at the point that the distinction must be made; a material point is not capable of consciousness or purpose, but a spiritual point is. Whether a spirit can be at the same place as a material point is a detail we need not settle; nothing depends on it.

The elementary material things may have dimensions, or may be points. Either way they are different from located spirits. We do not end up with a contradictory

---

[2] René Descartes, *Meditations on the First Philosophy* (Meditation VI), in the Everyman edition of *A Discourse on Method*, London, 1912.

[3] John C. Eccles, *The Neurophysiological Basis of Mind* (Oxford, 1953), chap. 8.

theory in which we are forced to conclude that located spirits are both material and non-material.

Located spirits are still methodologically elusive. But they are not subject to the other philosophical objections which have been urged against spiritual things.

(ii) Scientific Objections to Spirit

Spirit is supposed to be a very different sort of stuff from matter. The advance of our knowledge of living things, their evolution, development, and growth, raises difficulties for any theory of spirit.

The Continuity of Nature

There are two aspects of the continuity of nature which pose essentially the same question for spirits, the Problem of Evolution, and the Problem of Growth. Evolutionary theory asserts that complex modern forms, such as man, are the remote descendants of earlier species so much simpler that like the amoeba they show no signs of mental life. If minds are spirits they must have arrived as quite novel objects in the universe, some time between then and now. But when? We see only a smooth development in the fossil record. Any choice of time as the moment at which spirit first emerged seems hopelessly arbitrary.

In the embryonic development of man, the same problem arises. The initial fertilized cell shows no more mentality than an amoeba. By a smooth process of division and specialization the embryo grows into an infant. The infant has a mind, but at what point in its development are we to locate the acquisition of a spirit? As before, any choice is dauntingly arbitrary.

The continuity of mental with non-mental forms is capable of two interpretations. Continuity shows that men and one-celled organisms have the same basic nature, and we may conclude from this that since single cells are without spirit, so must be man. This is the materialist response, and is, I think, the more common one among zoologists. Alternatively, we may conclude from the common nature of men and amoebas that as men have a spirit, so must amoebas also.

The continuity of structure extends even further. The smooth sequence, in descending complexity, from one-celled animals through viruses and protein molecules to simple material groupings leads us either to a more confident materialism, or to the view that all matter shares with man his more-than-material nature. The second response is known as panpsychism, the doctrine that mind is to be found throughout nature.

The scientific difficulty for any form of dualism is therefore this; the continuity of nature leads a dualist inexorably on to panpsychism, but panpsychism is a speculation which extends the field of the mental far beyond anything warranted by the direct evidence of mentality.

And if we reject the continuity of nature by insisting that spirit did make a sudden appearance in the world, we must explain if we can how a non-spirited parent can have a spirited offspring, and by what mechanism a spirit is acquired by a developing embryo.

None of this can refute Dualism; after all, the world is full of surprises. Nevertheless, these considerations should make a thoughtful man uneasy. The reason why the Mind-Body problem is a classic in philosophy is that the alternatives to Dualism should make a thoughtful man uneasy too.

(iii) Interactionist Dualism

The most important and common form of Dualism is that which, following common opinion, affirms the interaction of body and mind.[4] This variant must therefore reject (4) Matter and spirit do not interact. It must accordingly confront the reasons advanced against interaction in chapter 2, and show them to be insufficient.

Spirit-Matter Interactions Are Anomalous

If spirits are conceived of as located, then at least changes in the brain bring about changes in a spirit at some definite place within itself. This slightly alleviates the oddity of the connection, but does not change the situation very much. And we can enlarge on how anomalous the connections must be.

If the dualists are right, events in the brain, of a complexity which defeats the imagination, can cause effects of great simplicity in the spirit. For example, the experience of seeing a red circle on a white ground requires brain activity involving millions of cells. And vice versa, so simple a mental event as deciding to go to bed sets in train, on the Dualist account, cortical events of the most staggeringly complicated sort.

[4] For example, Descartes, *op. cit.;* Michael Maher, *Psychology,* London, 1940.

Because no mechanism connects matter with spirit, such causal connections must be primitive, fundamental ones. In no other case are there fundamental connections between the simple and the complex. In no other case is the effect of a complex activity quite different from any composition of the effects of part of the complex. Matter-spirit connections, if they occur at all, are quite unlike any others. And unless panpsychism is true, they occur only in tiny fragments of the universe.

These anomalies must be conceded. But as we pointed out in chapter 2, to show that something is unusual does not show that it does not exist. Formally speaking, this is a sufficient defense of interaction against the anomaly criticism. We cannot decide about interaction by considering the anomaly alone. What matters is whether reasons in favor of interaction are strong enough to outweigh the anomalies. And that in turn depends on how satisfactory the alternatives to interactionist dualism can be made.

The Shadow of Physiology

Interaction is a two-way affair. If spirit acts on matter, then what happens in the mind must make a difference to what happens in the brain. Consequently, not every brain event can be determined solely by antecedent physical conditions and follow recognized physical laws.

Conversely, if all brain happenings are determined solely by physical influences operating on the antecedent physical condition of the brain, then spirit has no effect on matter. The Shadow of Physiology is the likelihood that this is so, and consequently, that interactionist dualism is false. For the only way out is a theory of Double Causation, according to which both spiritual and material conditions are separate but complete causes of some particular brain events. But this is a spurious way of escape, for Double Causation is an incoherent idea. Either the material and the spiritual were both effective (both made a difference), in which case each was part only of the cause and the physical causes are not complete, or one was idling and was not effective although it might have been. In that case the idling member is not a cause at all. If physiology is complete, then to introduce spiritual causes alongside physical causes and have one or the other idling all the time, is idle indeed.

So the question we must face is: How solid is the evidence that for explaining events in the brain, physiology is, in principle, complete? How dark is the shadow of physiology? In the previous chapter we saw the completeness of physiology as an extension of the successes of contemporary biochemistry. We suggested the shadow was pretty dark. Let us now make a further examination of the situation.

Before considering brain activity more particularly, we must notice that earlier, more general arguments from the conservation of energy are invalid. Let us admit that the body and its environment form an energy-conserving system, so the spirit neither supplies nor absorbs energy. As C. D. Broad pointed out,[5] changes in the distribution of energy, and hence causal changes, can be brought about without supplying

[5] C. D. Broad, *The Mind and Its Place in Nature* (London, 1925), chap. 3.

any energy. His example was the string and bob of a pendulum. The condition of the string is causally efficacious in determining the path of the bob, but supplies no energy to it. Jerome Schaffer's example,[6] illustrating the same point, is a radioactive atom. A spirit could cause it to disintegrate at a particular time, so changing the pattern of energy distribution, without supplying energy, and so without violating the conservation principle. As for the production of spiritual effects by material causes, it is no part of the conservation principle that the production of non-material effects requires physical energy.

Now let us turn to brain activity itself. D. M. Armstrong,[7] in his discussion of this question, assumes that unless there is a time-lag somewhere in the chain of physical events, the spirit would have no opportunity to act. In hitting a cricket ball, for example, impulses from the eyes affect the brain, and this in turn affects the spirit, giving us vision of the ball. The spirit next decides how to act, and then, after the period required for the spiritual events, the brain would change and so affect the muscles controlling the bat. If there is no waiting period in the chain of physical events, then there cannot be any effective spiritual activity. So far as I know, there is no evidence for such a delay.

Although a time-lag would be splendid evidence of spiritual action, this is not the only way in which spirit could be active. There is, after all, no time-lag within which the pendulum string acts on the bob, or the earth

[6] J. A. Schaffer, *Philosophy of Mind* (Englewood Cliffs, N.J., 1968), pp. 66–67.

[7] D. M. Armstrong, *A Materialist Theory of the Mind* (London, 1968), pp. 32–34.

on the moon. In the same way, the spirit could effect a general constraint upon physical processes which go on without interruption, affecting their course but not breaking in upon them. It may take no longer for the brain to enter the ball-hitting condition when the spirit is directing events than when the spirit is on holiday; so long as the end result is different, the spirit has been efficacious.

There is a further complication. The indeterminacy in quantum laws means that any one of a range of outcomes of atomic events in the brain is equally compatible with known physical laws. And differences on the quantum scale can accumulate into very great differences in over-all brain condition. So there is some room for spiritual activity even within the limits set by physical law. There could be, without violation of physical law, a general spiritual constraint upon what occurs inside the head.

Although many outcomes are equally possible within quantum laws, they are not all equally probable. So the evidence for spiritual constraint would consist in total brain activity deviating in a non-random way from the expected probabilities. Because we are ignorant of the detailed constitution and working of the brain, we do not know what these expected probabilities are. We do not know whether spiritual activity is affecting the brain.

Interaction of spirit and brain is not positively excluded by contemporary knowledge. Yet for most people researching brain function, the working hypothesis is that no such thing occurs. For in the absence of evidence to the contrary, the most economical and therefore best assumption is that only physical causes are at work. The interactionist dualist must bet that the economical assumption will prove inadequate to the facts. Until there is some sign of inadequacy, his bet is a baseless one, and hence one that in sound philosophy ought not to be made. There is at present no light by which we might dissipate the shadow of physiology.

(iv) Parallelism

If we abandon the interaction of matter with spirit, but cling to the dual character of man as having a material body and a spiritual mind, we become Parallelists. Parallelists may hold that neither matter nor spirit affects the other, or that matter can affect spirit but not vice versa.

The first alternative is that of the classical Parallelists in the tradition of Descartes, who accepted his dualism but could not admit any causal action across the border between matter and spirit.[8] They pictured the bodily and mental as occurring always in step, always parallel, but never linked by a causal tie. Thus, with M_1, etc., as mental events, and B_1, etc., as bodily events, and arrows indicating causal links:

$$\text{Mind} \quad \ldots \rightarrow M_1 \rightarrow M_2 \rightarrow M_3 \rightarrow \ldots$$
$$\text{Body} \quad \ldots \rightarrow B_1 \rightarrow B_2 \rightarrow B_3 \rightarrow \ldots$$

So that at the time when I become aware of the change in the traffic light (mental event), changes occur in the

[8] See, e.g., Malebranche, *Dialogues on Metaphysics and on Religion,* London, 1923, and Leibniz, *Exposition and Defence of the New System,* in *Philosophical Writings,* ed. Mary Morris, London, 1934.

brain (bodily event). The awareness leads to the (mental) decision to move off, the brain changes set in train the muscular operations involved in starting the car. The processes are so synchronized that it appears the mind and the body interact, but this is illusion. The processes are kept in step by a divine Pre-Established Harmony, like two synchronized clocks in Geulincx' image of the situation, which keep time without affecting each other, because they have been preset to do so.

A rowing crew illustrates the same idea. If we knew nothing of rowing and were watching the oarsmen from some distance away, the movement of the oars would suggest almost irresistibly a causal connection of one rower with the next. The oars keep time, accelerate and decelerate together, as if joined by connecting rods and so interacting. Yet this appearance of causal connection is deceptive. The rowers act independently. Their apparent connection springs from a pre-established harmony set up by training.

This form of Parallelism was always thought to be a last desperate resort. It involves postulating all manner of unsuspected hidden mental causes. If, for example, I am surprised by the pain I suddenly feel when (but not because) I step barefooted onto a carpet tack, there must have been some unconscious mental state preceding and causing the pain. This is an unhappy conclusion; the method clutters the mind with a host of new unconscious events.

Introducing the Pre-Established Harmony is likely to offend also against the canons of method. For anything which can explain such a harmony is likely to be capable of anything and so incapable of explaining why there is one sort of harmony rather than another.

The second form of Parallelism asserts that matter can affect spirit but is not affected by it.[9] Our picture is then one of bodily causes having both bodily and mental effects:

$$\text{Mind} \quad \ldots \; M_1 \qquad M_2 \qquad M_3 \qquad M_4 \; \ldots$$
$$\qquad\qquad\qquad \nearrow \qquad \nearrow \qquad \nearrow$$
$$\text{Body} \quad \ldots \; B_1 \rightarrow B_2 \rightarrow B_3 \rightarrow B_4 \; \ldots$$

If we deny that the mind is in any sense a spiritual *thing,* and mental events never cause other mental events, then we think of it as a mere succession of events of awareness, decision, feeling, etc., arising from bodily causes. Such a view is Epiphenomenalism, popular in the late nineteenth century.

In the second form of Parallelism the causal hypotheses are in rather better order. They involve appeal only to events which we can ascertain independently do occur. We can again believe that treading on a carpet tack causes pain.

Both forms of Parallelism, however, do violence to our conviction that mental conditions are effective in human behavior. Unless we decide beforehand that such causal connections are impossible, ordinary ways of searching for causes lead unambiguously to the conclusion that perceptions, decisions, emotions, and moods can all be causal antecedents of bodily action.

Interactionism and Parallelism are both in trouble, but any dualism must take one or the other form. In consequence, the bulk of recent thought on the Mind-Body problem has involved denying the dual character

[9] See T. H. Huxley, *Methods and Results* (London, 1894), pp. 199–250, and Broad, *op. cit.*

of man. As the materiality of the body enjoys massive scientific support, the spirituality of the mind has naturally been the favorite casualty. To theories which deny that the mind is a spiritual thing we now turn.

Chapter 4

THE BEHAVIORIST SOLUTION

In what is, broadly speaking, the materialist trend of thought in modern times, Behaviorists are the most radical. They deny that the mind is a thing at all, and so deny *a fortiori* that it is a spiritual thing. If the mind is not a thing at all, there can be no problem of how the thing which is a mind relates to the body or anything else. Behaviorism is more a dissolution than a solution of the Mind-Body problem as we have posed it.

(i) The Behaviorist Doctrine of Mental States

Behaviorists assert that a "mental" description of a man as intelligent, angry, seeing a traffic light, or in pain, is not a description of what some special part of him—his mind—is like. Rather, such descriptions tell us of that man's behavior and dispositions to behave.[1]

To say a man is intelligent is to say that his rate of success in solving intellectual and practical problems is higher than normal, that solutions come to him comparatively quickly and with little effort, that he has the disposition to learn more quickly and forget more slowly than common men, and so on. The "and so on" is

[1] For example, B. F. Skinner, *Science and Human Behavior*, New York, 1953, and Gilbert Ryle, *The Concept of Mind*, London, 1949.

crucial; mental predicates are typically "open-ended" in that they point to a whole cluster of dispositional traits which is not at any time finally crystallized. To say of a particular performance, for example, making a speech, that it is intelligently done, is to say that in it the speaker exercises and displays some of the cluster of dispositions which together make up intelligence. But just which dispositions belong to the intelligence cluster, and just which of these are displayed, is not definitely specified in saying the speaker shows intelligence.

The difference between an angry man and one who is not is that the angry man tends to shout, throw things, froth at the mouth, attempt to hurt the object of his anger, and so on. The man who sees the traffic light has the capacity to conduct his car in a way quite different from him who does not see it. Both tendencies and capacities are kinds of disposition.

Mental descriptions, on the Behaviorist view, are not descriptions of a man's mental part. They are descriptions of his behavior and his dispositions to behave. Differences between mental states are differences in these behavior patterns and nothing more.

The Psychological Vocabulary Is Not Eliminable

Although mental descriptions describe nothing but behavior and behavioral tendencies, they cannot be translated into purely bodily terms. We cannot dispense with mental terms and use only behavioral ones to mean just what the mental terms meant. Mental descriptions cannot be replaced by behavioral descriptions because the former are vague, open-ended, and speak of patterns of action, whereas the latter are specific, determinate, and mention particular acts.

"He is angry" cannot be translated into any finite set of descriptions of him shouting, tearing his hair, flushing, striking, or grinding his teeth, for "He is angry" speaks indifferently of some pattern of behavior, not exactly specified, in which some or all of these are more or less prominent ingredients, and in which there may be other, hitherto unrecognized "expressions of anger." Yet this failure of translatability does not show the mind is more than behavior. For neither can "He won the battle" be translated into any finite set of descriptions of carnage, confusion, and flight. Yet "He won the battle" applies, in a flexible and rather unspecific way, exactly to the physical events of motion, noise, life, and death which constitute the battle, and not to anything else. So equally, maintain the behaviorists, "He is angry" applies to the display we call angry behavior and to nothing else.

We cannot conclude, because mental terms are not dispensable, that they describe something spiritual beyond the body and its behavior.

There Are No Mental Objects

Behaviorism rejects the idea that the mind is a spiritual thing, and rejects it principally because there can never be the public human experience of spirits upon which alone the idea and knowledge of such things could be founded. For the same reasons, Behaviorist theory has no place for mental objects. Sometimes men are in pain, but this does not mean that there are things called "pains" which they have, feel, or are in.

Sometimes men have afterimages, but there are no such things as afterimages that they have or see. Pains, afterimages, pangs of remorse, are not placeless, impalpable objects. We can fully describe what is happening when pains or pangs occur using sentences which refer only to the man involved: The man is suffering, or in an afterimage-seeing condition, or in a remorse-pang-feeling condition.

Thus mental objects are abstractions, conveniences of thought and speech, not real entities. "I have a pain" is more like "I have a new hair style" than "I have a new puppy." "I see an afterimage" is likened to "I walk a mile" rather than "I walk a tightrope." Descriptions of men mentioning pains, afterimages, or pangs of remorse are not relational descriptions connecting men with pains, etc., but complex descriptions of the men's condition, mentioning events or processes but not relating one object to another.

This doctrine is extended to all the "contents of the mind," the thoughts, sensations, surges of emotion, etc., which we might be tempted to think of as inner, non-physical objects. The elimination of mental objects is obligatory for anyone opposing the spiritual view of mind, as we saw in chapter 2. As it so greatly reduces the number of objects in our account of men, it is very appealing for Dualists too. So the program to eliminate mental objects is almost common ground in the philosophy of mind.

Behaviorists alone are committed to the further view that descriptions of men as suffering, having an afterimage, etc., describe only the behavior, and tendencies to behavior, of the man in question. His verbal behavior pattern, what he is apt to say about himself, is naturally of cardinal importance in these cases.

(ii) The Mind-Body Problem and the Problem of Other Minds

Behaviorism is thus a clear, uncompromising, thoroughly naturalistic doctrine of man. It makes possible a most attractive treatment of the Mind-Body problem and furthermore, it disposes of another classical conundrum, the problem of how we know our fellow men are not mindless automata.

Behaviorism transforms our view of the Mind-Body problem. It portrays the traditional Mind-Body problem as just a confusion. The mind is not a thing related to the body; the relation of mind to body is the relation of activity to agent. The problem of the relation of a siren to its wailings is not a particularly deep, perplexing, and "philosophical" one. The only problem is scientific: How does the siren work? In Behaviorist doctrine, the philosophical Mind-Body problem gives way to the scientific problem: How does the body work in producing those behavioral manifestations which we describe in mental terms? And this scientific problem is to be solved in two parts, a developed psychology establishing the laws which connect stimulus and response in all the phases of human behavior, and a developed physiology determining the neural bridges between them. This transformation of the Mind-Body problem is most satisfactory, for it becomes a problem to which we can apply well-established research techniques.

The classical problem of Other Minds, the problem of how we know that others who behave as we do have minds like us, also becomes a pseudoproblem. Like the Mind-Body problem, it is generated by mistakenly thinking that the mind is a thing, and since it is not a bodily thing, that it is a spiritual thing. The problem of Other Minds then arises because it is so hard to know when spiritual things are present or absent. From the Behaviorist standpoint, the problem of Other Minds is simply the problem of whether other people behave, or are disposed to behave, in the ways to which the mental terms apply. And it is quite obvious that they do. Even those raising the problem of Other Minds admit as much, but go on to ask whether in the case of other people any mind lies behind their behavior. For Behaviorists the mind does not lie behind, but in, the behavior. They hold that the traditional problem of Other Minds is one with which we are not faced, and which we would be unable to solve if we were. The traditional problem cannot even be stated unless the behavioral analysis of mental descriptions is rejected.

The objections to Behaviorism are not objections springing from a faulty treatment of the Mind-Body problem or the problem of Other Minds. The shortcomings of the theory lie rather in its general doctrine of the nature of mind, and are of two chief kinds. First, Behaviorism offers a faulty analysis of those mental descriptions which do pertain to patterns of behavior, for it omits the causal element in mental concepts. Second, at least some mental descriptions refer to events and processes which are neither behavioral nor dispositional.

(iii) Behaviorism and Mental Causes

According to Behaviorist doctrine, mental events are behavioral events or events of gaining and losing dispositions to behave. So mental events are always effects of whatever causes human behavior, or dispositions to show such effects. A man's mental condition is not the cause of any of his behavior; it does not cause him to say or do anything. The connection of mind to behavior is too close to be causal. For the behavior—writing a poem, say—is itself a piece of mental activity. Nothing is the cause of itself. The wail is not the cause of the siren making a noise, it *is* the noise. When we say the siren is of the superloud variety we are not saying it is now being very noisy, nor are we attributing to it a mysterious, ghostly, and inaudible loudness which is the cause of its wail being noisy. We are attributing to an ordinary material object, a siren, the disposition to be, when sounding, noisier than most. The Behaviorists analyze "This man is arrogant" along the lines of "This siren is superloud," as attributing a behavioral disposition and involving no reference to states or events hidden inside him.

Mental descriptions only explain behavior in the sense that they describe a man's behavior in general terms. "Because he is arrogant" answers "Why was he so rude?" in the same way that "Because it's a superloud one" answers "Why is the siren so noisy?" The answer assigns the rudeness, or noisiness, to the class of normal happenings. It does not give the cause, either of the disposition to perform arrogantly (loudly), or of the particular rude (noisy) performance in question.

In Behaviorist doctrine, what is true here of arrogance is true of every mental state or event—pains, sensations, emotions, decisions, intentions, and so on. The entire group of psychological expressions refers to behavior and behavioral dispositions. Body relates to mind as Nureyev relates not to Miss Fonteyn but to his dancing.

A mental condition, as a disposition to a pattern of behavior, can of course be a cause of events, even mental events, in other people. "His arrogance made him abhorred," "Her hypochondria made her a laughingstock," "His carelessness resulted in his dismissal" are all acceptable in Behaviorist theory. What is out of the question is that mental events, processes, or conditions should play a causal role in producing the behavior which is a manifestation of *that* mental event, process, or condition. To call the behavior a *manifestation* of the mental state is already misleading. The behavior *is* the mental state, to the extent that anything categorical constitutes a mental state. The mental state is never a cause of its own behavioral elements, just as nothing is cause of itself. It is this restriction on mental states as causes which is relevant in what follows.

For this restriction is utterly out of step with our normal use of mental concepts. Arrogance is a particularly favorable case for Behaviorists. We might agree that "It was his arrogance which caused him to be rude to the milkman" is like "It was the trend of population to the city which made him abandon his farm" and thus wrongly ascribes as cause something of which the alleged effect is really a part. For myself, I consider that even in this favorable case the Behaviorist view is wrong. "It was his arrogance which caused him to be rude to his milkman (when he was given the wrong order)" seems to me much more like "It was the low level of brake fluid which caused the brakes to fail (when the pedal was pressed)," in which we speak of a relatively permanent "standing" condition within which a particular event triggered another particular event as effect.

But be that as it may, our regular employment of many other mental concepts is certainly causal. "It was the pain that caused him to cry out," "It was the flashes before his eyes that caused him to seek an oculist," "It was his decision to go swimming which led to his taking a towel from the cupboard," "It was his love of honor which caused him to enlist," "It was his jealousy that made him kill her."

All these sentences are perfectly normal, and all use mental concepts in perfectly standard ways. They show that as we ordinarily think about the mind, mental events and conditions and processes are at least the sorts of things which can be causes. Some philosophers go further than this, and hold that the mental ideas are themselves causal in character. They think "jealousy", like "poison", is an idea which cannot even be fully understood except in terms of the sort of effects jealous (or poisonous) things have. We postpone discussion of this further claim to the next chapter; here we need only note that both the view that mental events *can* be causes of their manifestations in behavior, and the view that their causal role is an integral part of the meaning of mental terms, are incompatible with Behaviorism.

The Behaviorists know this very well. They recognize that in common thought mental events are often held to be causes. They believe this to be a fundamental error, both deriving from and helping to prop up the Dualism with which common thought is infected. The error consists in mistakenly analyzing mental descriptions along the same lines as physical ones, so that just as "He built a house" describes a sequence of public events in a public space involving physical rearrangements, so "He built a fantasy" is thought to describe a sequence of private events in a private space involving mental rearrangements. The analysis of mental descriptions as parallel to physical ones lands us with both a spiritual mind and impalpable mental objects as its contents. The analogy of mental to physical descriptions may be tempting, but Behaviorists believe it tempts us to philosophical ruin. For mental descriptions, like all others, get the meaning they have from the circumstances in which we can know it is correct to apply them. Let us call these conditions "criterial conditions". The only criterial conditions for "He built a fantasy" are the behavioral dispositions, especially to verbalization, through which the subject passes. Mental descriptions, like all descriptions, claim that the conditions criterial for their application obtain; hence they do not, and cannot, refer to private events but to tendencies for there to be public and physical events. To suggest otherwise is incoherent, for on the alternative which construes mental descriptions as analogous to bodily ones, there will be no criterial conditions for the mental words, so they will have no meaning at all.

The position we have now reached is a very curious

one. Angry behavior is never caused by any of the commonly accepted causes; it is never caused by anger, or by the intention to seem angry, or by the resolve to play on stage the part of an angry man. Angry behavior has, under no circumstances, a mental cause. The common opinion is in error, not just as in thinking bad air gives folk malaria, where among possible causes the wrong one is chosen, but as in supposing that Newton's laws keep the planets in motion, where a cause of quite the wrong sort altogether is proposed. Contrary to our fond opinions, unless we know some brain physiology we are quite ignorant of what makes people behave as they do, except that in knowing what some stimuli are we can know what response to expect. To think pleasure or pain, hostility or admiration are ever operative factors in human life is to suffer an illusion generated by misunderstanding descriptions which use mental terms.

Nevertheless, we are not to suppose angry behavior has no natural cause at all. Nothing could be further from the naturalistic spirit of Behaviorism than to make human life a continuing miracle in which stimulus and response just happen to exhibit intelligible patterns. Nor are we to think non-physical causes are at work; the error in Dualism is not just taking the *mind* to be a spirit but in thinking there is an inner spirit at all which could be cause of behavior to which mental descriptions apply. No matter what terms, mental or otherwise, we use in speaking of the spiritual, these terms will be without sense. For they will lack public criterial conditions without which no terms have sense.

So Behaviorists hold that angry behavior has non-mental physiological causes. It springs, so we conjecture, from a special condition of the brain. But that special brain condition cannot be anger, for the existence of such a condition is no part of what we look for in seeking criterial circumstances for "He is angry."

Thus although in common life anger is thought of as a cause of angry behavior, and states of the nervous system are discovered, in developing science, to be a cause of that very same behavior, an argument from how mental terms get their meaning stands in the way of applying the mental term "anger" to the appropriate causes of angry behavior to be found in the nervous system.

Behaviorism thus involves revising our psychological vocabulary. References to the causes of behavior are transformed into descriptions of patterns in the behavioral effects themselves. There will be no need to make this radical change, and no point to it, if the argument from how mental terms get their meaning can be successfully challenged. And on the other hand, if the argument is sound, this will establish Behaviorism and confound all its alternatives. A challenge to the argument has been mounted in recent years, and this will be discussed in the next chapter.

Whether or not that challenge is successful, we encounter here one of the knottiest knots in philosophical method. A certain principle about how words and sentences get their meaning, and what meaning they get, has as consequence a very radical new conception of mental expressions. Should we conclude that since mental expressions do not have the meaning which the principle awards them, there is something faulty in the principle? Or should we conclude rather that, because our ordinary thinking has ignored a sound principle, there is just confusion and no real meaning at all in mental words as ordinarily intended? Whichever way we decide, how could we justify our decision to someone who disagreed?

(iv) Mental Episodes

The second group of objections to Behaviorism centers about mental episodes and claims that behavioral accounts of these are inadequate. Pains are favorite examples of mental episodes. To have a pain is, according to Behaviorists, to acquire a set of dispositions to move one's body in the pain-behaving way. Wincing, groaning, soothing the hurt part, taking aspirin, stiffening the upper lip, and a hundred other pieces of behavior all belong to the pain group, and to be in pain is to be disposed to exhibit a fair sample of behaviors from this group. Some elements of this group, such as bodily tension, are not properly under voluntary control, and so scarcely count as behavior rather than mere bodily happening. There is a general problem about what is behavior and what is mere happening, but we will pass it by. It will not matter to us if some pieces of the pain-behaving pattern are not, in strictness of language, pieces of behaving at all.

For the objection to this account of pain is that it leaves something out, something usually called the sensation of pain. We display our tendency to think of pain in this way as a definite inner episode by speaking of pain-behavior as our *reaction* to pain, suggesting that the pain is an event which triggers it off. And we may well feel that what the Behaviorists omit from their account of pain is the very thing which matters most about it. Pains hurt; indeed that is their most salient feature. But for Behaviorists, to have a pain is to acquire a complex disposition. On one view of dispositions, acquiring a disposition is just having come true some conditional statements describing my tendency to behave. Who can believe that the truth of some conditional statements can literally hurt? On another view of dispositions, the acquiring of a disposition involves the acquisition of some particular real inner state which underlies and serves to explain the conditional truths which describe my tendency to behave. It is indeed sensible to think such an inner state could be hurtful. But on Behaviorist principles the inner state could not be the pain. For the vocabulary of pain gets its sense from the criterial conditions for its application, and hence refers not to any inner state but instead to the very behaviors and behavior tendencies which we blunderingly call "expressions" of the pain. So that on the second view of dispositions we reach the crazy conclusion that even if something involved in having a pain could hurt, it would not be the pain but something else.

There is further trouble for Behaviorists in the problem of distinguishing real from imitation mental episodes. Consider this argument:

To have a pain is to acquire dispositions to pain-behavior.

To decide to imitate a man in pain is also to acquire dispositions to pain behavior, maybe the very same set of pain-expressing behaviors.

So having pains and deciding to imitate them are not different sorts of mental episodes.

Since pains hurt and decisions to imitate them never do, the conclusion is false, and therefore at least one of the premisses is false too. Behaviorists defending themselves against this argument must show that one or other premiss does not follow from their principles. They might point first to the presence of some involuntary conditions in the case of pain, for example, bodily tension, which are absent from the decision to imitate pain. This is an unsuccessful defense, for pains and their expert imitation will then be the same in the possible situation where every perceptible bodily happening is subject to voluntary control, and this is just as absurd. Second, it might be suggested that only a segment of the dispositions coincide. For example, the pain-sufferer will be urgently wishing this section of his life were over and done with in a way quite lacking in the pain-imitator. This defense is unsuccessful, for wishing gets in turn a behavior-disposition analysis, and the imitator can extend his imitation to the expressions of wishing, which include speaking, keeping diaries, sighing even when alone, and so on.

Third, there is the defense which fills out the analysis of pains, decisions, and mental episodes generally, by including mention of their causes. Pains are now not just dispositions to pain behavior, but dispositions caused by bodily damage or malfunction, while their imitations have a quite different set of causes. This is not a successful move, for it implies that someone who feels tickles when others feel pain (i.e., when there is bodily damage or malfunction), but is resolved to conceal this fact by an imitation of pain, really feels pains after all.

Those who attack Behaviorism maintain that not

only can there be pain-behavior without pain, there can be pain without pain-behavior or any disposition thereto. Thus Behaviorists are accused of the error of thinking a paralytic can feel no pain. It is more satisfactory to argue the question for normal people, so we must turn to less urgent sensations to make the point. A slight glow of well-being may have no behavioral manifestations at all, yet still exist and be felt. Alternatively, and this is equally fatal, its manifestations may be quite indistinguishable from those of a determination to please the boss by a smart and cheerful demeanor.

So Behaviorism is unsatisfactory in its treatment of the episodes called sensations. It is also unsatisfactory in dealing with episodes which occur in perceiving. When I see that the traffic light has changed, more has happened than just the acquisition of a new set of dispositions to acts in which I discriminate one state of the traffic light from another. If I have a curious sort of color blindness, in which I see as many different shades of color as you do, but different ones, then when we both see the traffic light (or anything else) we will each acquire the very same discriminative dispositions. Yet there are great differences in our mental lives, and since these differences cannot appear in a behavioral analysis, that analysis is unsatisfactory.

(v) The Strength of Behaviorism

Behaviorism, despite its great virtue in dealing with the Mind-Body problem, is deficient as a general philosophy of mind. Yet it expresses, in a distorted form, a truth of the first importance. This truth is that there is a conceptual connection between descriptions of creatures in mental terms and descriptions in behavioral terms. It is impossible to understand or explicate mental terms without some sort of reference to behavioral dispositions.

Excitement and fear are two different mental states. Yet by all subjective tests of introspection and memory, a case of excitement and a case of fear may not differ at all. What makes one excitement and the other fear are the different bodily activities associated with each.

Again, all the "inner" features of jealousy and hatred may be the same. What distinguishes them, what makes them the mental states they are, lies in the pattern of action belonging to each.

Again, no matter what it seemed like to the person who made it, a decision to marry would not be a decision to marry unless (hindrances apart), it were followed by some bride-seeking performances.

At least some mental conditions cannot be fully described without mention of bodily action. So there is some kind of logical connection between mental states and what happens in and to the body.

Behaviorism takes the extreme view that mental descriptions describe, imprecisely and obliquely, nothing but behavior and tendencies to behave. It reaches this view by way of the principle that unless mental descriptions refer only to the behavioral "expressions" of the mental state described, they can have no meaning at all. It thus restricts the reference of mental expressions to perceptible conditions for their proper application. Since the manifestations of a mental state are the only aspects of mental life which we can see, hear, or touch,

Behaviorism identifies a mental state with the pattern of its manifestations.

The Mind-Body problem thus leads us on again into the fields of metaphysics and epistemology. For now we must ask: Is there any way of retaining the conceptual link of mind with behavior while denying that the subject matters of mental and behavioral descriptions coincide exactly? If so, is this new position compatible with human limitations on understanding and knowledge? Affirmative answers to both questions will occupy us in the first part of the next chapter.

Chapter 5

CENTRAL-STATE MATERIALISM

(i) The Causal Theory of the Mind

Some terms get their meaning by reference to the effects produced by what the terms denote. Take "poison", for example. No one understands what a poison is if he doesn't understand that drinking it is not a good idea. It is in terms of its deleterious effects upon human or animal health that we express what "poison" means. There is a conceptual connection between poisons and ill-health. Yet talk about poisons is not just talk about ill-health. It is talk about substances which can play a *causal role* in ill-health. A poisonous substance will, if swallowed in large enough doses, without any inhibitor, by a person who takes neither a neutralizer nor an emetic, and provided his metabolism is typical, adversely affect his health.

Arsenic is a substance quite separate from humans, healthy or otherwise. It is a poison whether swallowed or not. Yet although arsenic is something different from humans and health, when we describe it as poisonous we are adverting to its connection with illness and death. "A poison is apt to produce illness and death" is like "A furnace heats"; it is a statement specifying conditions under which a substance deserves the label "poison" ("furnace"). By contrast, "A poison tends to deteriorate if left standing" or "A furnace burns more fuel if the draft is forced" do not deal with what must be so if the label "poison" or "furnace" is deserved.

We explain what a poison is by reference to health, but not to deterioration if left standing. "Poison", we can say, is an *essentially causal term*. Through this causal element, poisons and health are conceptually linked although they are different things.

Some terms apply to objects not in virtue of what the objects cause, but in virtue of what played a part in causing them; terms like that could be called *essentially effectual terms*. For example, "sedimentary rock" or "pig iron" can be explained only by reference to how such rock or such iron comes to be produced.

The Causal Theory of mind likens most mental descriptions to "poisonous", but appeals occasionally to the other pattern shown by "sedimentary rock".[1] A decision to go swimming, for example, is held to be a state of the person tending to cause going-swimming behavior, that is, behavior from the wide and vague collection: assembling swimming gear, asking others to come swimming, going to a beach, filling the pool, swimming, etc. As in the case of poisons, we must add qualifications when we say the appropriate effects will be produced. The decision will not issue in going-swimming behavior if I am paralyzed, or have an accident on the way, or change my mind, or am ordered by my superior officer to remain on duty. Nevertheless it is not just a matter of fact that your decisions to go swimming typically issue in your going swimming. The decision earns its title to the description "decision to go swimming" because it is a mental state which tends to have precisely that effect.

So too with, for example, "seeing a cricket ball". A man who sees a cricket ball is a man who is in a

[1] See, e.g., Armstrong, *op. cit.*

state which, if circumstances are favorable, has a characteristic range of effects: catching, dodging, striking the ball, warning people in its path, directing those searching for it, applauding the batsman, etc., etc. We can call effects in this range "cricket ball discriminating behavior," and say that seeing a cricket ball is a mental state which is both essentially effectual—it is produced by the action of a cricket ball upon the eyes—and essentially causal—it is a condition of capacity for cricket ball-discriminating behavior. It is only a capacity for such behavior. The capacity is not necessarily exercised; the sight of a cricket ball may give rise to no discriminating behavior whatever.

A capacity is a disposition; the Behaviorists were right to emphasize how heavily dispositional much mental description is. The Causal Theory of mind appropriates that lesson of Behaviorism. Mental states are typically states with a causal role in disposing men to certain forms of behavior; so runs the Causal Theory.

An itch is a cause of scratching, a tickle of giggling, a pain of wincing. Emotions are causes of characteristic patterns of action: rage of shouting, jealousy of poisoning, envy of denigrating, joy of singing. Moods do not have dispositions to characteristic activities as effect, but are modifying causes: there is a recognizable style in the behavior of an anxious man no matter what he is doing; he behaves, as we say, anxiously, rather than indulges in any special sorts of action. On the Causal Theory of mind anxiety is an inner state which affects the manner in which he conducts himself. And the same goes for hope and desperation.

To describe a man as intelligent is not just to say with the Behaviorists that he is apt to turn in an intelligent performance, a performance in which more problems are solved more readily and more adequately than is typical for men. It is to say that an inner structure or condition of the man is an indispensable immediate causal factor in producing the intelligent performance, and that this inner condition is what is rightly called intelligence. "Intelligence" names not the performance-pattern but one part of its cause, the inner and therefore mental part.

Sometimes the connection of mental state to behavior is more indirect. In thinking, for example in deliberating upon what to do, mental states of belief and supposition lead not straight to behavior but to other mental states, inferred or concluded beliefs, which may then govern action at some much later time. And the opinions I form in deliberating may never be given a behavioral manifestation because situations in which they would be operative in controlling behavior never arise. Yet according to the Causal Theory, all mental states can, directly or through the mediation of other mental states, cause the person who has them to pursue one course rather than another in the conduct of his life.

Thus the Causal Theory of mind has two strands: that the various mental events and processes are postulated causes of segments of behavior belonging to various recognizable patterns, and that the mental causes are given their names in virtue of their postulated connection with those behavior patterns. The first strand admits the view that the mind is something inner, separate, and standing behind behavior. It thus allows for the existence of definite, non-behavioral, non-dispositional mental episodes and states, and so avoids one chief problem of Behaviorism. It also allows (indeed insists) that mental states are causally efficacious in behavior, and so avoids the other chief problem.

The second strand, that mental terms get their meaning by reference to the behavioral effects of the mental states they denote, preserves the truth of Behaviorism that there is a conceptual connection of mind with behavior. But the connection between them is not that of referring to just the same facts.

The Causal Theory of mind views mental concepts as theoretical. The picture it paints is this: Men, confronted with the surprises of human (and animal) behavior in comparison with the activities of water, earth, and trees, have surmised that something inside them is causing their distinctive conduct. This something, of which little is known but its causal powers, is called a mind. And the mind is credited with as much complexity as there is complexity and difference in the characteristically human behavior of men. Talk about mental characteristics is talk in terms of a theory (the theory of minds) about what makes men tick.

Little is known, in this primitive stage of theorizing, about what a mind is: is the cause of behavior a demon in the breast, a soul dispersed throughout the body, a spirit without any spatial features, or a plastic box two inches behind the nose? It is a task of scientific theory-development to find out. The conceptual analysis of mental descriptions leads to *a* cause within the man, but leaves open what kind of cause it is. Defenders of the Causal Theory of mind liken "mind" to "gene". Men, struck by the surprising fact that for the most part cattle, sheep, sweet peas, and fruit flies reproduce offspring after their own kind, have surmised that something passed from parents to offspring is causally responsible for the offspring's development into a creature resembling its parents. There are as many genes as there are distinct hereditary characteristics. A gene is something which causes offspring to resemble parents in, say, eye color. Talk about genes is talk in terms of a theory (the theory of genes) about what makes children like their parents. It is talk in terms of *a* cause for the phenomenon of inheritance. Discovering what the cause actually is (a special DNA molecule in the cell nucleus) is a scientific triumph in theory development which no amount of reflection on statements of genetic theory will accomplish. The same holds for the mind.

(ii) The Significance of Mental Terms

The Causal Theory of mind requires an extension of the limits placed by positivism on the conditions under which terms are significant. Positivism restricts the content of a term to perceptual features in conditions to which it applies. A general positivism, provided it grants that bodily movements are perceptible, leads directly to Behaviorism about minds. By contrast, the causal account of minds depends upon an epistemology of postulation. The epistemology of postulation admits as significant terms which apply to postulated causes, which may be imperceptible, of perceptible features in the world. This extension not only allows the philosophy of mind to escape its Behaviorist fetters, it permits a much more satisfactory philosophy of micro-objects in scientific theory, and a much more realistic philosophy of God, of the past, and of what is hidden in the depths of the sea.

The argument to Behaviorism from positivist restrictions on the significance of mental terms has to my mind been successfully challenged by the more liberal epistemology of postulation. The way is open to explore less paradoxical accounts of what a mind is, and the Causal Theory is a very promising one of these. To give a sample of its promise: the mental causes of behavior may be causes of which we are not conscious; on this view the unconscious mind is not at all scandalous or impossible. Whether or not we have such a thing is just a question of psychological theory.

Again, the Causal Theory of mind allows that not all the properties of the mind must be mental ones. The mental properties are those relevant to the causation of behavior. But that which causes behavior can have a host of other properties as well, for example, warm or cool, moist or dry, which are not referred to in describing the mind as governing behavior. In breaking the idea that every property of the mind must be distinctively mental, the Causal Theory breaks one of the strongest prejudices supporting a Dualist bifurcation of the world.

Self-Awareness

The comparison of minds with genes reveals, however, a very great peculiarity of minds. Minds are supposed to be hypothetical, hidden, inner causes of behavior. Yet in our own case they may be inner, but are certainly not always hypothetical or hidden. Some mental episodes, mental states, and mental processes are given to us in self-awareness or by introspection. A fit of anger and a pang of remorse are not in our own case hypothetical events proposed to explain the experienced movements of our bodies. They are themselves items given to experience. They are given, of course, not to perception, but to the inner awareness whereby we know, without the use of sense organs, some of what is going on in our own minds. Such mental events are not theoretical; they belong to the data, not to its explanation.

Here the Causal Theory is given a subtle and ingenious turn. Why is there such difficulty in giving any full description of these mental episodes and conditions? Why do they prove so elusive to introspective research? Why are we so ignorant of their true nature and relations? The answer given is that we are aware of inner states only as causes more or less like each other. All I know, when I know I am having a fit of anger, is that a cause of throwing, gnashing, and abusing, directed at some person or group, has come to existence in me, that it is stronger or weaker than others, and that it is already producing bodily changes, for example, flushes, clenching, or shivering. In a slogan, we can say: Introspective knowledge is knowledge of causes. Introspective awareness is awareness only of the causal properties of an event or state. The awareness is in turn a mental state, and it also, insofar as it is mental, has causal properties. In this case, the causal properties give us a capacity for discriminative acts.

In its attempt to accommodate the facts of self-awareness, the Causal Theory of the mind thus exploits the transparent character of inner awareness, and the way that awareness continually points beyond the mental state to the associated action.

Inner knowledge is, according to the theory, direct

knowledge of causal powers, which we have learned to recognize in the course of growing up. Whether there can be introspective knowledge of a mental state's causal powers without any associated knowledge of its intrinsic qualities is hard to say. Such knowledge is certainly unusual, but then introspective knowledge is unusual in all sorts of ways, so why not in this?

Survival of Death

The idea that a man's mind survives the death and dissolution of his body is older than history. It seems to make sense at least to most people, whether or not they share the ancient hope in another life. Here is another way in which the Causal Theory of mind is closer than Behaviorism to common modes of thought. For the Behaviorist, mental life without sense organs and limbs is a flat impossibility. If the description of a man as having solved a problem in mental arithmetic is a description of the bodily responses to which he has become disposed, then of course the bodiless man, who is not disposed to any responses whatever, cannot solve problems in mental arithmetic. The same goes for any and every mental description. They all apply solely to bodily actions and dispositions to such actions. Disembodied mental life is ruled out by the Behaviorist analyses of mental concepts.

The Causal Theorist is not so radical. He holds that our descriptions of mental life are descriptions of inner states typically effective as causes in bodily action. A Causal Theorist can be a Dualist. He can hold that the inner causes are states of a spiritual thing which could survive bodily death. If the surviving spirit had the illusion that it was still allied with a body, it could not only do mental arithmetic, it could decide to go swimming or to do anything else without any absurdity. After death these states could continue to be, but their descriptions as causes of behavior will no longer be apt. They would be rather like arsenic in a lifeless world: there as much as ever, but not quite poisonous any more.

In Central-State Materialism, as we shall see, the mind whose states are causes of behavior, is held to be itself a part of the body. Being part of the body, it dies and disintegrates along with the rest of the corpse. So in Central-State Materialism, although survival of death is a possibility, it turns out not to be a fact.

The fact of survival would thus refute Central-State Materialism, but would not destroy the Causal Theory of mind. Judging the survival question requires a philosophical review of the scientific evidence and rational argument for survival, and of special ways, like religious revelation, whereby we might come to know such a momentous fact. It deserves a whole book to itself: but I share the majority view among contemporary philosophers, which rejects the claim to survival. If this is the correct view, the denial of survival is not a fault in Central-State Materialism.

(iii) Central-State Materialism

The Causal Theory of mind sets up a scientific task: to find what in a man is causally responsible for those facets of his behavior which are "expressions" of mental conditions. When that task is complete we will have a full doctrine of what a mind is, and not just a causal schema which mentions some cause or other but does not fully specify it.

It is now universally accepted that in this connection the brain and its appendages are the bodily parts which matter most. If any bodily part is the thing whose events and processes are causes of behavior, the central nervous system is that thing. Central-State Materialism thus affirms the Causal Theory of mind and adds that behavior can be completely explained in terms of events in the central nervous system. The mind, the cause of behavior, turns out to be the brain.

One more step is required to reach Central-State Materialism. This step insists that the nervous system has no properties of a non-physical kind.[2] It insists that the only properties the nervous system has are the properties recognized in chemistry and physics, together with their derivatives. Without this step the doctrine is not a materialism but a theory which accords to the brain two different sorts of attributes, non-material as well as material ones. Such a view is compatible with the Causal Theory of mind whether or not the non-material properties are described in terms of their part in the causation of behavior. If they are, they would be mental properties of the mind. If they are not, they would belong to the mind but not be mental properties, like having a temperature of 98.4°F.

Central-State Materialism is thus the most uncompromisingly economical version of the Causal Theory of mind. It identifies the cause of behavior as a purely

[2] See Brian Medlin, "Ryle and the Materialist Hypothesis," in *The Identity Theory of Mind,* ed. C. F. Presley, Brisbane, 1967.

material object, the central nervous system as conceived in neurophysiology.

Central-State Materialism and the Mind-Body Problem

Central-State Materialism does not, like Behaviorism, deny that the mind is a thing. But it does deny that the mind is a spiritual thing. So Central-State Materialism solves the Mind-Body problem by denying the second of our four incompatible propositions.

More fully, the answer concerning the relation of mind to body is: the mind is part of the body. It is a special part, the part which controls behavior. That is, it is the part which governs the movement of the limbs under the influence both of its own states (e.g., purposes) and of sensorily gained information concerning the body's environment and attitude. The part which does this is the brain, whose connections are chiefly with sense organs, which affect it, and muscles and glands, which it affects.

Thus the Mind-Body problem resolves into one of scientific detail. In precisely what changes does the brain play a part, and what part does it play? Neurophysiology is the science which will furnish the full account of the relation of mind to body. The relation of mind to *matter* is already settled: a mind is a special arrangement of matter in an organism, which is another special arrangement of matter. It is not some different non-material sort of thing standing in mysterious relation to the matter which makes up living bodies.

Just as there is no specially philosophical problem of the relation of a bus to its engine, and no special

Boat-Rudder problem or Pump-Refrigerator problem in philosophy, so there is no special Mind-Body problem beyond the scientific one of the causal interplay of elements in a system. Considered as a solution to the traditional problem of mind and body, Central-State Materialism is highly satisfactory.

As in the case of Behaviorism, the objections to Central-State Materialism lie not in its solution of the Mind-Body problem, but in its general doctrine as a philosophy of mind. Let us note first some problems which, like survival, are problems for materialism but not for the Causal Theory of mind on which it relies.

Free-Will

Central-State Materialism involves a particular solution to that great philosophical problem, the problem of the Freedom of the Will. Consider a decision to go swimming which is promptly and effectively acted on. I decide to go swimming, and forthwith do go swimming. We would normally think of my swimming as freely done. In swimming I exercise my freedom. Nothing and no one forced me to go swimming. This does not mean that my swimming had no cause. It was not a freak of chance that I ended up in the water. My swimming was free in that it was my decision, an act of my own mind, which set my body off in the direction of the water. The decision is an act of choice between various alternatives.

Now some philosophers insist that the choice must itself be free if my swimming is to be an exercise of freedom. And they insist further that if the choosing is an effect of antecedent conditions outside myself it is not really free. For it has been determined in advance, by factors over which I have no control. For example, the state of mind described as fondness for swimming has been established in me by natural processes, and is now there whether I wish it or not. Likewise, recognizing that I now have an opportunity to swim is a mental state which just occurs, willy-nilly. If factors like these operate as natural causes which combine to result in my choosing to swim, then my choice is really beyond my control. But a choice beyond my control is not a free choice.

Philosophers who argue this way conclude that the only action which is genuinely free stems from choices for which there are no adequate natural causes. Let us call causeless choices of this kind *metaphysical choices*. On this account, men are free only if they sometimes make metaphysical choices.

How does this affect Central-State Materialism? A metaphysical choice is, or leads to, a brain state which sets activity going. This brain state is not caused by any earlier conditions of the brain or anything else. So not all brain states come into existence as effects of physical forces. Hence, if there is metaphysical choice, Central-State Materialism is false.

Whether or not men are free, and whether freedom involves metaphysical choice, are great questions which must be tackled on their own. Here we must be content to notice that Central-State Materialism is compatible only with some restricted concept of human freedom according to which some choices, although they are the determined effect of many natural causes, are nevertheless free.

Parapsychology

Parapsychological phenomena, by definition, demonstrate capacities of mind which exceed any capacities of brain. The brain is receptive only to information which arrives by neural pathways, and so is confined to perception by way of the senses. If some people can learn more about distant, hidden, or future fact than memory and inference from present sense perception can teach them, then their minds are not just brains. Such extra knowledge is said to be gained by extra-sensory perception, precognition, or more generally, clairvoyance.

Again, the brain is capable of receiving information about the mind of another only by perception of the other's body, bodily acts, effects of such bodily acts, and perception of reports from yet other people. If some minds are receptive to the contents of the mind of another by some more direct means (telepathy), then those minds are not just brains.

If some minds display psychokinesis, that is, can move physical objects by act of will, without use of natural or artificial limbs, and not by exploiting the weak electromagnetic field in the head, then such minds can do what no brain can do.

If some minds are capable of surviving the death of their owners and then temporarily controlling the behavior of a person still living, as the "controls" of trance-mediums are sometimes alleged to do, then these surviving and displacing minds cannot be mere brains.

If even a single example of any of these types of para-

normal phenomena is genuine, Central-State Materialism is false. The difficulty in parapsychology is to produce unequivocal evidence that any part of it is genuine.
Each type of phenomenon is open to a serious doubt
of one kind or another. Psychokinesis was the
speciality of the so-called "physical mediums" who
flourished roughly from 1880 till 1935, and has been
the subject of dice-rolling experiments, since then. According to the reports, the physical mediums levitated
objects, made them fly through the air, switched
switches inside intact soap bubbles or locked metal
boxes, overturned furniture, and so on. Not all the
effects can be explained, or ever will be. However, all
the mediums subject to thorough investigation were
caught cheating sooner or later. And in really tight
conditions of experimental control, when trickery is
very difficult, the results were almost always meager.
The shadow of doubt cast by the discovery of fraud is
a wide one, for if some of a medium's effects are the
work of known deceptions, it seems likely that his other
effects are produced by unknown deceptions. But it
would not be fair to rush to a conclusion. If the reports
are to be trusted, many events have occurred for which
no normal explanation seems possible, let alone has
actually been found.

The psychokinetic experiments on controlling the outcome of rolling dice, conducted at Duke University
under J. B. Rhine, are open to severe methodological
objections, and their positive results cannot be taken to
establish anything significant.

The "mental mediums" were those who, in a trance
state, performed feats either of telepathy with the living
or communication with the dead. There are two prob-

lems in establishing that such performances are genuine. First, it must be shown that the information produced by the medium was absolutely unavailable to her through normal channels. This is a task of the utmost difficulty. The medium cannot be monitored for her whole life to establish just what she has learned, and how. The spectacular retrieval of "forgotten" knowledge under hypnosis shows just how cautious we must be before ruling out books and newspapers read long ago, chance conversations, or the use of barely perceptible clues in accounting for the surprising and correct information mediums sometimes produce.

Further, it must be shown that the successes of the medium are of such a kind, so frequent, and so detailed, as to rule out the "null hypothesis", the idea that a medium is just a lucky guesser. And it is a dauntingly difficult project to produce any satisfactory quantitative measure of the level of success a medium must reach to establish her *bona fides* as a paranormal person. We can of course recognize some performances which would be utterly convincing. If the medium could produce, without ever failing or erring, information which would lead to the discovery of previously unknown facts about any named dead person, famous or obscure, ancient or modern, Christian or Hindu, a reasonable person would be convinced. Doubt would still exist whether this was communication with the dead, clairvoyant knowledge of the evidence, or precognitive telepathy with the investigators subsequently confirming her claims. But whichever of these processes were occurring, it would be paranormal and so sufficient to refute Central-State Materialism. Unhappily, no medium reaches such an unambiguous standard. They all err, stumble, and produce commonplace and guessable truths as well as notable surprises. Mental mediums are not (yet) able to produce satisfactorily convincing evidence for so large an hypothesis as the existence of psychic powers.

The attempt to introduce experimental control into the study of telepathy and clairvoyance has given rise to the tradition of card-guessing experiments in psychical research. Here it is possible, by randomizing methods, control of the experimental conditions, and statistical analysis, to rule out the alternative of normal access to the information, and to measure the extent to which the rate of success exceeds what is to be expected on the null hypothesis, the hypothesis of pure chance.

A few experimental series, involving a few subjects and experimenters, have produced results diverging from chance expectation so far as to refute the null hypothesis. There remains only the question whether the subject achieves his success by normal methods. C. R. Hansel, the chief skeptical critic of parapsychology, has made a study of all the best experiments in the Western world, and pointed to opportunities for conscious or unconscious cheating in every one of them. He does not rely on the ever present possibility of publishing results which were never obtained. This requires a conspiracy to defraud on the part of whole teams of people. Hansel is concerned with ways in which a single person taking part in the experiments could have produced the reported results by normal means. In the famous Soal-Shackleton series of experiments, he can only find ways of cheating which require the cooperation of at least two people. Nevertheless, he is able to point out that the results fell back to chance level on those occasions when Soal took no part in the experiments, and when Shackleton was tested by a different team in South Africa he produced no significant scores.

L. L. Vasiliev, working in Russia, has obtained significant results in experiments on the production of hypnotic sleep over a distance, without perception, to a subject isolated from radiations of every known sort. Not even Hansel, that most ingenious deviser of ruses, can fault the experimental methods used.

Repeatability and Fraud in Parapsychology

The Mind-Body problem requires for its solution a judgment on parapsychology, and that in turn raises general questions in philosophy, and in particular, in epistemology. We must confront the problem of how evidence can have weight, and this raises the question of fraud. The problem of fraud is that we know men can, and do, cheat and dissemble, but we do not know that they have paranormal capacities. On the contrary, the great weight of our fully attested knowledge of man's origin and constitution makes paranormal capacities extremely unlikely. So for any result in psychical research which can be explained either by appeal to paranormal powers or by the hypothesis of fraud, the explanation by fraud is the more rational one.

If the paranormal results can be obtained with only one set of people, who have an interest in the success of the experiment, on one occasion only, fraud cannot be ruled out. This is true even if we cannot think how the trick was worked. It is easier to invent a trick than to detect it.

Only repeatability can eliminate the hypothesis of fraud. If the subject can repeat, or nearly repeat, his paranormal feat for anybody, at any suitable time, in any suitable place, under conditions which any independent experimenter is free to vary at will, with assistants whom the experimenter can choose, then fraud can be excluded as an explanation of the events.

This kind of repeatability is demanded, and obtained, for experimental results in other scientific fields. Results which other experimenters cannot duplicate (or nearly duplicate) are excluded as arising from some unknown distorting influence, improper conduct of the experiment, or fraud. Unrepeatable results cannot be used to establish anything.

It is important to realize that repeatability is not necessary for something to *be* genuine. If the best jumper ever to live reaches his peak and then suffers an accident, the highest jump ever made will not be repeatable. But of course this does not mean that it was never made. Equally, perhaps only one man on one day of his life was in communication with the dead. The fact that he is unable to repeat the feat does not mean that it never happened. But it does mean that we cannot have proper evidence that it happened. Repeatability is not necessary for a phenomenon to be genuine, but it is necessary for us to have a well-founded belief in its reality. The reason for this lies in human unreliability.

I think it is fair to claim that so far, no paranormal results have been satisfactorily repeatable. So I conclude that although parapsychology could in principle refute Central-State Materialism, the researches so far fail to do so.

Even if some paranormal results were established as

genuine, they might of course be accommodated in a new, expanded, physical science. Here we must recall the relativity of materialism mentioned in chapter 2. Television is paranormal with respect to Newton's physics, but not to ours. The fact that some neomaterialism might survive the establishment of paranormal truths would not vindicate Central-State Materialism. For Central-State Materialism is a materialism based on our present physical and chemical science. If that science is inadequate, the materialism based on it is false. The doctrine that some science, we don't know at the moment which, is adequate to support a Central-State doctrine of the mind, is so vague and so weak that it is not worth holding or discussing.

(iv) The Causal Theory of Mind Examined

There are two strands in Central-State Materialism, the doctrine that the mind is the cause of behavior, and the doctrine that the central nervous system, being the cause of behavior, is the mind. Survival, freedom, and paranormal powers are threats to the second strand, but do not touch the first.

The Causal Theory of mind states that descriptions of mental events, states, and processes are descriptions of inner conditions insofar as they are, directly or indirectly, causally efficacious in the behavior of an organism. This is a simplified statement of the view. Some states, for example, having dream images, are described not as themselves causally efficacious, but as resembling other mental states, perceptual ones, which do have a real role in governing behavior. But images are exceptional; the simplified formula captures the heart of the mind. Whatever else the mind is, matter or spirit, electric or chemical, it is a field of causes, and all its distinctively mental properties prove to be causal ones.

There seems to me no doubt that there is a conceptual connection, a connection of meaning, between mental and behavioral descriptions. It also seems plain enough that mental descriptions cannot in general be dissolved into statements of behavior and behavioral disposition without leaving something essential out. Further, we constantly employ mental categories in expounding the causes of human behavior. The Causal Theory of mind retains the vital conceptual link with behavior, gives to mind an independent existence as an inner something whose states are typically causes of that behavior, and so accounts for our natural employment of mental terms in causal explanations.

A doctrine with which it is hard to quarrel is that in our very understanding of what a mind is there proves to be an idea of the inner causation of behavior. The mental states, whether states of a spirit or states of a brain, will of course have many properties, of location, extent, physics, and chemistry (or mayhap spiritual machinery) in virtue of which they are causes. A state cannot be a cause and have *no* other properties; such a "pure cause" is just magic. But the Causal Theory of mind maintains that none of these other properties are mental. They do not enter into what we mean in any description of a state of mind as a state of mind. It is like a political description of an electorate. The electors are described by eligibility to vote, number, division into districts and wards, party affiliation, and so on. The electors are also men and women, short and tall, slim and stout. But sex and size do not enter into the political descriptions of these people. Similarly, only as causes of behavior do properties of inner states count as mental. The mental description, according to the Causal Theory of mind, encompasses only description as cause.

The crucial question, therefore, is: Is the mind, insofar as it is mental, nothing but a field of causes? Are the only genuinely mental properties of inner states causal properties, or similarities to states with causal powers?

Pains Again

In urging the deficiencies of Behaviorism, we argued that the theory could not cope satisfactorily with the fact that pains hurt. How does the Causal Theory of mind fare in dealing with this question?

Being in pain is a complex condition. Suppose my finger is burned, and is painful in consequence. In my mental state there are at least two components: awareness that my finger has been overheated, as a result of which it is still damaged, and a peremptory desire that this awareness should cease forthwith. In this present discussion, both the awareness and the desire must naturally be given a causal analysis.

"I am aware that my finger has been burned" is analyzed as "As a result of having been burned on the finger, I have entered a new inner state apt to produce behavior wherein I discriminate the burned finger from others which are not burned." In the discriminating behavior I not only favor the correct finger, I favor it in the burn-soothing way. That is, I give verbal and active expression to the belief that my finger has been burned.

So far so good. But the hurtfulness of the burn has not yet been captured. All that has so far been said would be true even if burns did not hurt but throbbed. Instead of the whole range of bodily sensations we in fact enjoy or endure, tingles, tickles, itches, searing pains, jabbing pains, aches, feelings of numbness, etc., suppose we only ever felt throbs. The frequency of the throbs could differentiate different bodily conditions. One throb per second in the finger would signal a burn, two a cut, three an itchy mosquito bite, three and a half a tickling feather, and so on. Then in our case of the burned finger, the whole of the above analysis of "I am aware that my finger has been burned" would be true, and the episode would not be one which hurt in the slightest.

Or again, suppose a being very like us except that instead of feeling a pain when he burns his finger or breaks his toe, he has no locatable sensations at all. He just spontaneously gains a new belief, it just "pops into his head" that he has burned his finger or broken his toe, as the case may be. Call this being an *imitation man*. His awareness of his own body would be like our awareness that the car we are driving in is getting a flat tire. Some change in our body, of which we are not conscious, has as a result that it just pops into our heads that the the tire is going flat.

Awareness of the kind we have, that our finger is burned, ceases at the end of successful soothing operations. The bare belief of the imitation man that his finger has been burned could just disappear in the same way, as our belief that the tire is flat evaporates when we change the wheel.

The imitation man satisfies the analysis given above of "I am aware that I have burned my finger." But his pains do not hurt. There is nothing essentially hurtful, indeed no element which can be hurtful, in awareness of damage or malfunction as that awareness is analyzed by the Causal Theory. So the hurtfulness of pain must lie elsewhere.

Does it perhaps lie in the desire that the awareness should cease? Pains are unpleasant. We prefer not to have them. We often think that we prefer not to have them *because* they are hurtful. But perhaps this is a mistake. Perhaps their hurtfulness is precisely that we desire to be rid of them. Consider in the following how desire appears in a causal analysis.

"I desire to be rid of this condition of finger-burned awareness" is glossed as "I have entered an inner condition driving me toward (apt to produce) general expressions of pain, such as grimacing, together with whatever behavior I believe likely to minimize or eliminate another inner condition, my awareness of my burned finger." In everyone, this condition leads to wringing the hand and trying to cool it. In sophisticates like us, it leads further to searching out the burn cream, the analgesics, and even the doctor.

The strength of my drive to minimize awareness of my burned finger is the extent to which this purpose excludes or overrides all my other inner causes of behavior, and this varies directly with the intensity of the hurt. This is a point in favor of the idea that the desire is the hurtful element in pain. If conditions A and B increase and decrease together, then perhaps A and

B are the same condition. If they vary inversely, or independently, then they must be different conditions.

Nevertheless, there seems to be something wrong with the idea that a desire, understood as a cause, could be the very thing which is hurtful. What is hurtful must be something felt, and we can see that a causally understood desire is not something felt by considering other cases.

An urgent desire, causally understood, is an inner condition which, temporarily suppressing other causes of behavior, generates a pattern of bodily activity. A condition of this kind can be induced by hypnotic suggestion. A subject can be given an urgent desire, which is to say, an overmastering drive toward one particular behavior pattern, and it is clear from this case that such an inner cause is not something which, as cause, can be felt. So it is not something which can hurt.

We can also see that the causal analyses of awareness and desire in pain fail to capture the hurtfulness of pains by considering the possibility of the transposition of pains. Suppose a man for whom burning pains and crushing pains were transposed, so that when his finger is burned he feels as we do when our finger is crushed, and vice versa. The causal analyses of the elements in pain make his situation and ours exactly alike. He is aware that his finger has been burned, and so are we. He is gripped by the purpose to minimize the inner condition of awareness, and so are we. He works this purpose out in grimacing, handwringing, cream-applying, etc., and so do we. On the causal analysis of mental states, his state and ours are identical. Yet he is being hurt in the feeling-crushed fashion, and we are not. Our mental states are not identical. So the causal analysis leaves something out, something which distinguishes burning from crushing pains even where a transposition of pains makes their causal properties identical.

We might try to save the causal analysis by further complicating the picture of pain. Neither the awareness that my finger is burned, nor my desire to be rid of this awareness, is itself anything hurtful. But in pain I am not only aware through bodily sense of the condition of my finger; I am also aware, by introspection, that I am aware of my finger's condition. So we might suppose the element of the pain situation which involves suffering is this inner awareness.

Or alternatively, we could hold that the hurtful state is my introspective awareness of the desire that my bodily awareness of my burned finger should cease.

Neither of these strategies is successful. For the introspective awareness they invoke must itself be given a causal analysis. It is in its turn no more than the entering of a third new inner state enabling discriminative behavior—largely verbal behavior—toward the original states of bodily awareness and consequent desire. And once again, the description of this second, introspective, awareness as enabling discrimination leaves undescribed the hurtfulness which distinguishes us from the imitation man, who can perform this kind of introspection yet cannot suffer. So once again the hurtfulness of the burn in general, and its particular burning hurtfulness, elude a causal analysis of the mental concepts. Everything the causal doctrine can say about pains is true of the imitation man whose pains never hurt.

Although it is a very difficult matter, I believe the same general criticism holds in the case of the different perceptual states involved in seeing different colors, or smelling different smells, or, on the emotional side, undergoing different kinds of fear, fright, shock, and thrill. The causal doctrine covers well the description of mentality by one observing and explaining his fellow men. But the theory leaves out, to put it briefly, what waking life is like to him who is living it.

(v) The Causal Theory of Mind Amended

The criticism leveled above at the Causal Theory of mind can be expressed in this way: The peculiarly "mental" features of mental states are not all of them causal properties respecting behavior or similarities to causal properties. There are, in addition, characteristics of some mental states which especially concern how those states seem to him who has them. Thus there are the burning, jabbing, throbbing, and aching sorts of pain; the salty, bitter, sweet, and avocado-like sorts of taste; the different experiences of seeing things as variously colored; the different feelings involved in different emotions.

Let us accept the existence of these additional, noncausal features of mental states, and let us call them *phenomenal* properties. What follows for Central-State Materialism from the existence of such phenomenal properties? The Causal Theory of mind is important for materialism because purely causal descriptions of a state are *ontically neutral*. That is to say, a purely causal description of a mental state begs no questions about what sort of state it is, claiming only that it is causally operative in producing an organism's behavior.

So far as causal description goes, a mental state could be a state of a material thing, or a spiritual thing, or even a divine thing. The Causal Theory of mind leaves open, for scientific investigation to close, the question of what sort of thing a mind is. Philosophers who adopt the Causal Theory and go on to say scientific investigations indicate that the brain, a material thing, is the object whose states are causes of behavior are of course Central-State Materialists.

But Central-State Materialism is not automatically refuted if the Causal Theory is inadequate. If any property is ontically neutral, it is of course possible for a material object to have that property. So the mind can be an entirely material object even if mental states have phenomenal properties, provided the phenomenal properties are also ontically neutral. If phenomenal properties are ontically neutral, the Central-State Materialist is not embarrassed by their existence.

To see whether phenomenal properties are ontically neutral, let us return to the burning pain in my finger. The pain is a discrimination-enabling change in my mental state which sets up a desire for its own elimination. This change is in fact a change in the pattern and frequency of discharges of neurons in the cortex. But I am not aware of all this flurry of neuron firings *as a flurry of neuron firings*. Suppose, however, that I am aware of it as a condition which hurts. I do not grasp the brain-process clearly in its full reality, or in its reality at all. I grasp it, obscurely, in the guise of the painfulness of the pain. Nevertheless, it is this brain process, and not something else, which I grasp. To suffer is, on this account, to introspect rather clumsily a process which is itself material.

The phenomenal properties are not, on this view, properties of things as they actually are. They are how certain inner properties, which are both material and mental, appear to him who has them. They belong not to the reality, but to the appearance, of mental states.

Whatever belongs to appearance only is ontically neutral. It might have been some state of an indwelling spirit which, in suffering, I clumsily introspect. But it proves, so the argument runs, that the states set up in me by burning my finger, are brain states, and hurting is how these states seem to the organism enduring them.

The doctrine for hurting, that it is a merely apparent and not a real property, is then generalized to cover all phenomenal properties. So they are all ontically neutral. And as a result, even if we amend the Causal Theory and admit phenomenal properties, Central-State Materialism survives intact.

For a considerable time, I found this view very attractive. But I no longer think it acceptable. It is all very well to claim that hurtfulness is how activity of the C-fibers in the cortex appears, that the smell of onion is how the shape of onion molecules appears to a human with a normal nasal system, that scarlet is how a surface reflecting a certain pattern of photons appears to human vision. This deals with the pain, smell, or color apprehended and, relegating it to the category of appearance, renders it ontically neutral. But it leaves us with a set of *seemings,* acts of imperfect apprehension, in which the phenomenal properties are grasped. So we must ask the new question: Is it possible that things can *seem to be* in a certain way to a merely material system? Is there a way in which acts of imperfect apprehension can be seen to be ontically neutral?

Consider a camera. A green tree can certainly be within the field the camera can photograph. And with color film, the camera produces a negative from which a photograph of a green tree can be made. We can say if we wish, although it is stretching words a bit, that the tree appears to the camera, and even appears to the camera as green. A fancy camera is made which develops and prints its own film once exposed, and we could say of this camera that at exposure it enters an inner state apt for the production of green tree photographs. Especially if the developing process varies with the color of the tree, this is a simulacrum of green tree-perceiving behavior. And it is stretching words rather less to say that the tree appears as green to the fancy camera.

Even so, this is not the sort of *appearing to* that we are concerned with. We want to insist that the camera does not experience anything at all. For all its tricks, we do not think it makes a vast difference to the fancy camera whether its shutters are open or closed. We do not think this makes the world seem a very different place, for we do not think that to the camera the world seems to be any sort of place at all. With us it is different. Whether our eyelids are open or closed makes a great difference to how the world seems. It is this difference which is in question when we ask about the ontic neutrality of the awareness of phenomenal properties. Sensitivity to various environments and differential reaction to these environments do not suffice to account for the world's seeming thus and so.

Materialists sometimes argue at this point that the

difference between an experiencing man and a non-
experiencing self-developing camera lies in the simplicity of the one and the complexity of the other. The
man is sensitive to a whole range of conditions whose
variation makes no difference to the inner state of the
camera. The man has memory, and purposes, and
emotions, of which the camera is innocent. In the man,
a whole host of feedback mechanisms monitor his
activity. I do not find this appeal to complexity convincing. Think again of the imitation man, who duplicates
all of a typical man's acquisition, processing, and retrieval of information, and all his activity, but for whom
there are no phenomenal properties.

If the imitation man's finger is burned, he knows
that something is going on in his finger. And he knows
further that there is activity in him by which he knows
this. The further activity is in fact activity of the
C-fibers, but he does not know that that is what it is.
He apprehends it imperfectly, as we do, but he does
not apprehend it *by suffering,* as we do. He just knows
it, as we just know when we are awake, for example,
that whatever inner condition it is which marks off
waking from sleep is present within us.

The imitation man can know sea and sky are alike
in color, and even call them "blue". So can a blind man.
Unlike a blind man, the imitation man can find it out
for himself. When he looks at sea or sky he forms the
belief that what he is looking at has the color which
he has been taught to call "blue". Yet the imitation
man does not see the sea and sky *as blue.* He is not
able to enjoy their color, for they do not appear as
colored to him. Similarly, he can tell when his finger
is burned or crushed, and have a powerful drive to elim-

inate the condition by which he knows this. Yet he cannot suffer.

So far as I can see, imperfect apprehension can be kept ontically neutral only so long as it is analyzed solely in terms of what is known. So long as it is given that sort of account, the imitation man's imperfect apprehension is no different from ours. The difference is not in what is known but in how it is known. The materialist account of real men can find no place for the fact that our imperfect apprehension is by phenomenal property and not by, for example, beliefs just spontaneously arising.

I do not see how the ontically neutral descriptions available to the materialist can cover more than what is true of the imitation man. But I have not proved that this is impossible. Failing conclusive argument, we must just judge as best we can how adequate the materialist treatment of awareness by phenomenal properties can be.

Chapter 6

FUNCTIONALISM

In recent years the Causal Theory of the mind has been developed and refined into an account of the mind known as Functionalism. Functionalism's starting point is the view that when we use mental vocabulary (of perceiving, thinking, and acting, for example), we are describing episodes in terms of the functions they perform, as they mesh together, in establishing a person's goals and the ways that person goes about reaching those goals.

What makes a particular mental process a case of *perceiving,* rather than remembering or wondering or supposing, or deciding or longing? How the process is set going by a certain sort of cause (stimulation of the sense organs), and how the process then produces new belief, and perhaps surprise or satisfaction, and how it results in appropriate activity, by taking into account the information about the environment gained through the sense organs. Remembering can have much the same content as perceiving, but its role in a person's life is different: it is produced in a different way and issues in quite different patterns of behavior, since what is remembered need not be the present situation.

All this is part of a Causal Theory of mental terms. Functionalism stresses that mental states have two sorts of effect. Where they are present, then (typically at least) they modify behavior. Furthermore, they also typically result in the alteration or creation of other mental states, which in turn have their impact on our goals and how we seek them, by shaping behavior and creating further mental states in turn.

Functionalism is the theory that a causal account of this type gives the basic meaning of *all* the ordinary psychological terms. But it does not stop there; it holds that we can analyze complex mental processes in terms of sub-elements which are *themselves* functional. So Functionalism provides a research strategy for psychology. We start with a roughly described and imperfectly understood mental description, for example *conversing in English.* This can be given a first, crude, functional diagram, as appears on page 112.

The boxes in the diagram represent sub-units of the whole complex process, and each has a *functional* name, which describes the particular task it performs. The aim of functionalist psychology is to take each of these functional units (boxes) and show how it could perform its function if it were in turn composed of functional sub-units. For example, we might try to analyze the *memory* involved in conversation, and there is a simple illustration of the idea on page 113.

Then as a further step the functional sub-units in the Rememberer can be subjected to the same kind of analysis, revealing further sub-sub-units which function as simpler participants in the complex overall performance. The idea guiding functionalist psychology is that this process of functional analysis can be carried on to the stage where the sub-units involved are so simple that we will be able to understand the mechanism by which they work, and we could look for such mechanisms in the nerve tissues of the central nervous system.

The working assumption that the mental functions are

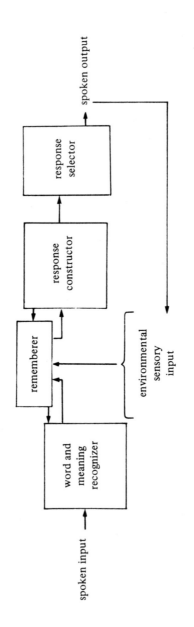

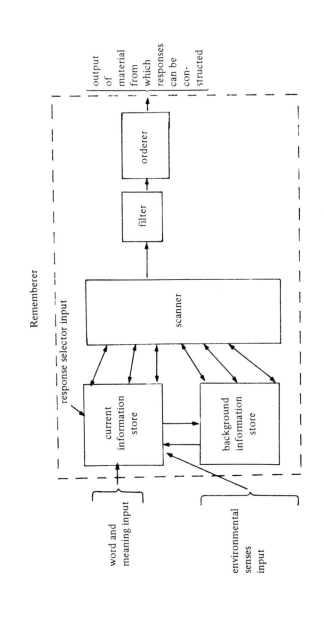

performed by the nervous system is what gives Function-alism its connection with Materialism.

(i) Artificial Intelligence

A functional conception of the mind has also been fostered in recent years by the development of computer technology, and in particular the investigation of Artificial Intelligence, or AI, which involves machines capable of recognizing and solving problems of ever-increasing difficulty.

Computer hardware can handle and manipulate infor-mation once it is transformed into a code of on/off signals which then exist as electrical impulses in the circuits of the machine.

Work on AI falls automatically into a functional form: the problem facing the researcher is to build a machine able to perform some given task, that is, to perform a function. And the researcher will not solve the problem without working out in detail *how* the task is to be per-formed. That involves finding the combinations of sub-units the machine must have if the whole machine is to perform properly.

The sub-units process information: they have inputs, which change the internal state of the sub-units and which the sub-units in turn transform into outputs. Their function is specified by describing what information they receive as input, how that information changes them, and what they do with it. This is a functional description, and the use of functional descriptions in the case of *artificial* intel-ligences quite naturally encourages and supports the idea that our understanding of *natural* intelligence, and other naturally occurring mental realities, will be improved if we can find out how functional sub-units fit together to perform the overall function in question.

So the Causal Theory of the mind is taken over in Functionalism and given further development. *Overall* causal patterns which concern inputs and outputs in the environment outside the whole organism define our everyday mental terms. In Functionalism these terms are analyzed, the further the better, into sub-units which are themselves described in terms of causes, of inputs transformed into outputs. For the sub-units we may have no everyday names at all, and the way they prove to fit together may involve many surprises and lead us to revise many of our everyday ideas about people and their minds. In this way a Functionalist philosophy of the mind can develop into a more detailed, scientific theory.

(ii) Materialism and Chauvinism

Central-State Materialism combined the Causal Theory of the mind with the claim that the various mental states and processes turned out to be different sorts of states and processes of the central nervous system. Types of mental state were identified with types of nervous state. But identity is symmetrical and reversible, so on this theory, unless a being has the right sorts of states and processes in the central nervous system, it does not have *any* mental states or processes. And a consequence of *that* is that only human beings with orthodox internal workings have minds. The theory has as a consequence that only normal people can think, or remember, or hope, or feel, or solve problems.

Perhaps that overstates the case; perhaps chimps and dogs will turn out to have brains sufficiently like humans to count as having mental states like us too. But even so there is an offensive arrogance about the idea that any being has a mind only to the extent that it matches humans in its internal workings. This arrogance seems totally unjustified when we consider intelligence in other creatures, and it has been called "human chauvinism." This is a deliberately disparaging description, for the current view is that any acceptable theory of mind must avoid the consequence that mentality is a human monopoly.

The development of Artificial Intelligence has been one powerful stimulus here: if something made of silicon chips and copper wire can perform as well as a human in some mental activity, of calculating, discriminating, problem solving, or diagnosis, why deny that a mental activity is indeed involved? What matters for the possession of mental characteristics is not *what you are made of,* but *what you do and how you do it,* that is, how you receive information from the environment, store it, manipulate it, respond to it, and make use of it in coherent activity.

This idea, that it does not matter what material construction is involved, because the possession of mental characteristics depends on function, is reinforced when we consider other possibilities. Suppose we met Martians with a highly advanced civilization, with language, literature, and technology. Would it be reasonable to deny that Martians have minds because they are built on different principles—their life based, perhaps, on the chemistry of silicon rather than carbon? Suppose we found that although showing every sign of high intelligence, some undersea creatures depended on a system which worked in a different way from ours, using tiny valves in a developed network of blood vessels, perhaps, instead of electronic impulses between nerve cells. That would not show that their intelligence was not genuine.

We can avoid human chauvinism if we allow that functional descriptions are sufficient for the possession of mental features. It is the function that matters, and the underlying physical (or even spiritual) structure which makes the functions possible can vary from case to case. Intelligence in humans, dogs, machines, and Martians is defined in terms of what the creature does, not how it is constructed, and human intelligence does not have any special status just because humans have a particular construction.

Thus the relationship between state of mind and inner bodily (or even spiritual) state is no longer one-one, as the identification of mental states with human brain states required. The relationship can be one-many, keeping open the possibility that similar mental states can be embodied in many different sorts of physical or spiritual stuff and structure.

When the one-many relationship of the mental to the physical has been recognized, it can be taken a step further. The fine detail of how your nervous system performs can differ from mine. You and I may well have developed in such a way that we use slightly different areas of the brain, linked up through slightly different pathways, in remembering that Columbus crossed the Atlantic in 1492. And we may make use of this knowledge through slightly varying operations within the total central nervous system.

Functionalism takes that in its stride, while it could embarrass a strict Identity Theory of the relation of mind to brain.

This development of a theory of one-many relationship between mental states and their physical embodiments is often called the shift from type-type to token-token identification. We no longer identify each different sort (type) of mental state with just one type of material state. Rather, each individual case (token) of a mental state— Napoleon being angry at the battle of Waterloo, for example—is an individual case (token) of a material state. But the material states corresponding to different cases of anger need not be all alike. Anger in people, in bees, in whales, and in Martians can have different physical bases, and yet all still be anger. But every actual case of anger is, so it turns out, a physical state. In this way Functionalism is held to hold no Dualistic or non-Materialist implications. Functionalism, like the Causal Theory, is *compatible* with either Materialism or Dualism. But it turns out, most Functionalists claim, that every mental *token* turns out to be a material, rather than a spiritual, state of a creature. Type/type identity fails. That is the lesson of avoiding human chauvinism. But token-token identity holds, so the physicalist vision of life and mind is not abandoned.

Actually, to restrict ourselves to token/token identifications, to go absolutely case by case in seeking the relation of mind to brain or its equivalent, will not quite work. To fully understand any being with a mind, Napoleon for example, we would need to track down what was *always,* every time he was angry, the corresponding state of his nervous system. Likewise for *all* the times he remembered Josephine. And so on. So in place of the *more general* types *anger,* or *remembering,* we need, not tokens, but *more specific* types, *anger in Napoleon, remembering in Napoleon, anger in the largest elephant in the London Zoo,* etc. Our hope and our guess is that many, if not all, of these specific types will turn out to be very like each other, even if not exactly alike. And in that case we will be able to build up sciences of psychology and physiology which will be able to grow closer together. On the Functionalist Theory of mentality, however, each will keep its own identity, and they will not be reduced to a single science, since function and composition are always distinct.

(iii) Embodiment and Supervenience

There is another way in which Functionalism has further developed the Causal Theory. Functionalism holds that the essential aspect of any mental description is its account of how input alters an inner element of the organism, and so changes the organism's behavioral output and dispositions to behavior. So mental descriptions deal in causes and effects, relations between the organism and the outside world, working through the inner structure we call the mind.

Brain descriptions, on the other hand, do not take this form. Basic anatomical brain descriptions deal with what the brain is made of, what parts it has, and how they fit together. Further, physiological brain descriptions describe the mechanisms at work in it, and how they proceed.

So mind descriptions and brain descriptions differ in what they set out to do, and the mental or brain characteristics described differ accordingly. Mental characteristics are causal and functional, while characteristics of tissue in the central nervous system make the mental functions possible but are not functional themselves.

So the idea of *identifying* mental and brain characteristics has given way to the better idea of seeing mind and brain related as function and what embodies the function, that is, what provides the physical means for the function to be performed. The model used to illustrate this comes from machinery. In car engines the function of lifting valves is often performed by a camshaft. So camshafts are often valve lifters. But the description *valve lifter* is functional, and the description *camshaft* is not. Rather, it specifies the material basis, the particular shape which enables a piece of steel to perform the valve-lifting function, and so specifies the *embodiment* of valve lifting in this particular engine.

Being a valve lifter is not to be *identified* with *being a camshaft*. Not all valve lifters are camshafts, and vice versa not all camshafts are valve lifters (some are oil pumps, for example).

In the same way, brain and mind are not thought of in Functionalism as strictly *identical*. Rather, mind is *embodied* in brain. That is the Materialist version of Functionalism: every mind, and every aspect of mind, is embodied in brain or some other physical structure. The same sort of mental state can have different embodiments in different creatures, or even different individuals from the same species, as we have seen. This means that psychology (which describes mental functions) cannot be reduced to some particular physiological description:

psychological knowledge is knowledge of the functions, while physiology deals with their embodiment.

Nevertheless, if every aspect of mentality has a physical embodiment, Materialism is correct. On the other hand, if no physical embodiment can be found for some mental features, then Dualism or some other alternative to Materialism must be the truth.

If mental descriptions do not mean the same as physical ones, as everyone agrees, and mental characteristics cannot be identified with physical ones, as Functionalism holds, what is the relationship of mental characters and their physical embodiment? The answer is *supervenience.* The mental is supervenient upon its embodiment. (If Materialism is true, that embodiment is always physical, as the word "embodiment" itself suggests.)

What does it mean to say that one characteristic supervenes on another? It is best to look at an example: The beauty of a painting is supervenient on its arrangement of patches of colored paint. So if two paintings are exactly alike in their arrangement of patches of color, they *must* be alike in beauty also. Two paintings cannot differ in beauty without differing in some other way also. Or again, it is impossible to change a painting from one that is not beautiful into one that is without *also* changing the arrangement of colored patches. The beauty of the painting arises out of and depends on the arrangement of colored patches in these ways, and we say that beauty is therefore supervenient.

Functions supervene on their embodiments in the same way. If two camshafts are alike in size, shape, and composition, and if they are both placed in the same situation in similar engines, then if one is a valve lifter, so is the other. It is impossible to convert a camshaft from a valve lifter to a non-valve lifter without changing its size, shape, composition, or relation to other parts of the engine. Being a valve lifter supervenes on being a camshaft in the appropriate place. And functional processes, such as *pumping oil,* or *remembering,* or *planning to invade Russia,* supervene on processes going on in the function's embodiment, such as *a piston moving down a cylinder,* or *all the neurons in a certain piece of brain firing in a certain special order.*

If all mental properties are functional, then they are all supervenient on their base. Although such functional properties are not reducible to the properties of their base, they do not introduce any new independent sort of being. If the base is always physical, then Materialists are right, and the mind does not involve any kind of substance different from the body.

(iv) Strength and Problems of Functionalism

Functionalism represents a development of the Causal Theory, with the advantages that human chauvinism is avoided and the relation of mental to bodily characteristics clarified. Through the relationships of supervenience and embodiment Functionalism shows how Materialism could be correct even though mental descriptions and psychological laws cannot be reduced to physical ones. So Functionalism in its Materialist version is the strongest form of Materialism yet developed.

Its problems are of two kinds: first, *are* all mental characteristics functional? And, do all mental functions have a purely physical embodiment? On the first question, it is the sensory qualities which give the most difficulty. What was said about pains for example, in discussing the Causal Theory in the previous chapter can be urged again here. For it is far from clear that the particular quality of a pain, as burning or stinging, for example, can be analyzed along functional lines in terms of patterns of stimulus and consequent change in inner state leading to altered resultant behavior.

On the second issue, the chief stumbling block is to show that *every* aspect of, for example, consciously imagining a theatrical scene by understanding a description of it can be captured in the information-processing capacities which nervous tissue does definitely embody. Do the formation of images, and conscious understanding, pass beyond this physical base and call for some more-than-physical, spiritual embodiment? If so, we will be back with the difficulties of Dualism.

The next and final chapter takes up the issue of phenomenal sensory qualities and discusses one way of treating them if Materialism is inadequate.

Chapter 7

A NEW EPIPHENOMENALISM

In chapter 5 we argued that although mental states are indeed inner causes apt to produce behavior, this is not all they are. Mental states have also, among their mental properties, phenomenal properties; and it was urged that awareness by phenomenal properties is incompatible with a purely materialist doctrine of the inner, mental causes of behavior.

So the position we reach is this: some bodily states, namely some states of the brain, are mental states. That is to say, they are causes of particular forms of behavior. And provided that neurophysiology is in principle complete, the only properties of the brain relevant to their role in causing behavior will be physicochemical ones. But these brain states have a complexity beyond their physical complexity, for some of them are also awarenesses of phenomenal properties. The grasping of such phenomenal properties resists material reduction, even though the causal role of such states does not.

To have a painfully burned finger is not just to encode burned finger information, to initiate burn-soothing behavior, and to encode in an imperfect apprehension that both these processes have occurred. It is also to suffer a burning hurtfulness. To be so suffering is a property of the man not reducible to his physics. As it occurs only when he is in a particular brain-state, it is best to hold that suffering pain is in the first place a property of his brain-state, and hence secondarily of the man as a whole.

The account given of awareness by phenomenal properties is the only point where the new Epiphenomenalism diverges from Central-State Materialism. Perhaps the new Epiphenomenalism could be called Central-State Materialism Plus.

If the brain's activities of a physical kind all occur in accordance with physical laws, suffering a burn, tasting the sweetness of sugar, or smelling the piquancy of cloves are processes in which the experience of the quality in question is inoperative in behavior, even the behavior in which such experiences are described. It is other aspects of the total state which play the operative part in setting the tongue in motion. The new Epiphenomenalism is therefore rather paradoxical in its account of the causation of behavior. To preserve the completeness of the physical accounts of human action, it must hold that, contrary to common belief, it is not the hurtfulness of pain which causes me to shun it nor the sweet taste of sugar which drives me to seek it. Strictly, it must be physical features of the processes in which awareness by phenomenal property is involved which have any effect on what I do. Whether we suffer or enjoy can be a sign that a given state is aversive or attractive for us, but cannot be a cause of aversion or attraction. To insist that it is a cause, in the present context, is to deny that the nervous system operates by purely physical principles. It is to turn from Epiphenomenalism back to some form of Dualism.[1]

---

[1] It may be a Dualism, not of things, body and mind, but of physical and mental properties of the same thing, the body. See, e.g., Ernest Nagel, "Are Naturalists Materialists?" in *Logic Without Metaphysics*, Glencoe, Ill., 1957.

The enjoying or enduring of phenomenal properties are called *epiphenomenal* characteristics for two reasons. They furnish the intrinsic content of sensibility. And although produced by what produces brain-states, they stand outside the causal chains linking stimulus to response.

(i) The Old and New Epiphenomenalisms

The doctrine labeled *Epiphenomenalism* which flourished in the nineteenth century also held that the causation of behavior was an entirely physical affair. But it denied the title *mental* to any state of the body, reserving that title for spiritual objects, experiences, which came into being when bodily conditions were suitable. These experiences had no effect on the course of a man's activity. This doctrine makes the mind an impotent side show to the serious business of real events in the physical world. It denies that mental events can be causes of behavior. It robs us of any satisfactory way of specifying different mental states, for this must be done through the links with behavior which the theory denies. It makes the Mind-Body problem wholly insoluble and makes it impossible to know if anyone, besides ourselves, has a mind at all.

So it is a most unattractive view, and was indeed only embraced because it alone seemed to allow for the completeness of physical explanations of what occurs in the physical world.

The new Epiphenomenalism, by contrast, holds that some bodily states are also mental states, and that the causal mental properties are physical properties of these bodily states. It insists only that the enjoying or enduring of phenomenal properties is not a physical affair. The new view allows, indeed requires, that mental states be causes, and allows, indeed requires, that different mental states be distinguished by reference to their differing links with behavior.

In contrast with the old, the new view denies that an epiphenomenal character is essential to the concept of a mind. On the new view, but not on the old, the inner states of the imitation man, which never have an epiphenomenal side, are nevertheless states of mind.

(ii) Double Aspect

One common view of the mind is called the Theory of Double Aspect. This theory holds that mental states have an "outer" aspect, revealed to normal scientific investigation, under which mental states are states of the brain, and also a second, "inner" aspect, in which they are known to introspection or self-consciousness.

This theory is ambiguous. It might amount only to a doctrine that there are two ways of knowing about mental states, an outer way by perception and instruments, and an inner introspective way. This is perfectly true, but it is also perfectly compatible with Central-State Materialism, which maintains the same doctrine.

The Theory of Double Aspect on the other hand might mean that mental states have two sorts of properties, one physical sort accessible to perception and photography, and another sort, accessible only to an inner, introspecting, mental sort of eye. This is sometimes, but not always, the case. Take an example from bodily sense; knowing where my left foot is. This is a state of which "outer" investigation by, for example, electroencephalographs may one day tell us a good deal. And "inner" introspection can assure us that it is present. That is, we can just know, without research, that we know where our left foot is. But introspection yields us no knowledge of any property of the state *knowing where my left foot is* which is not just a causal property equally accessible, in principle, to outer investigation. Like our knowledge that we are awake, our knowledge of where our left foot is does not involve apprehension by a phenomenal property.

There is another alternative too. In recent years P. F. Strawson[2] has propounded a view of mankind which attempts to by-pass the traditional questions of the relations of mind to body. On his theory two different sorts of properties, one sort shared with inanimate objects, such as *having a certain weight,* and the other peculiar to objects with minds, such as *being depressed,* belong to the very same thing, a person. His account of the mental properties is not causal; the analysis they are given is typically in terms of behavioral dispositions plus conscious-experience. The mental properties involve their bodily expressions, but are not reducible to material properties in either the Behaviorist or the Materialist way. They are properties of the body, although since the body is not *just* a body, it is called a person. His view is thus one form of Double Aspect theory.

Strawson's doctrine is distinguished from other Double Aspect accounts insofar as he identifies the whole

[2] Strawson, *op. cit.,* chap. 3.

body, and not some special part of it, as the bearer of the irreducible mental characteristics. His view is a Double Aspect theory twice over; there are two sorts of properties which persons have, and the mental properties of persons have both a behavioral and an experiential aspect.

The Mind-Body problem certainly takes a different form when Dualism is abandoned, but Strawson has offered no opinion on the causal connections between material properties and those aspects of mental properties which are experiential rather than behavioral. So the introduction of the concept of a person will not by itself dissipate all problems of how the mental and the physical relate in men.

The phenomenal properties we do experience are not necessarily non-physical ones accessible only to introspection. They may be physical conditions imperfectly apprehended. We need a theory of Double Aspect only if the particular kind of imperfect introspection which occurs in real men is not describable in materialistic terms. The new Epiphenomenalism is therefore a theory of the Double Aspect of some mental processes. Those mental processes which involve awareness by way of a phenomenal property have a dual aspect; they have two sorts of property, material and non-material.

The duality is not fundamentally the duality of public and private, which is a duality concerned with how properties can be known. The fact that a non-material process is not publicly discernible is only accidental. If men were gifted with a suitable, wide-spread telepathetic power these processes would be public, yet they would still not be material. Conversely, it is possible to suppose a physical property which could be discerned by only one person who suffered a unique defect of color vision. This property would be private, yet material.

(iii) The New Epiphenomenalism and the Mind-Body Problem

The new Epiphenomenalism leaves the Mind-Body problem in a rather curious condition. It divides the problem into two parts, one soluble and the other insoluble. It reaches different conclusions on different aspects of mentality. It challenges one of the assumptions of homogeneity, mentioned in chapter 1, in terms of which the problem has traditionally been raised.

The central truth about minds is their causal role in behavior. With respect to all the causal aspects of the mind, the Mind-Body problem takes the form: What is the relation between human bodily activity and its mental cause? And the answer is as given in Central-State Materialism: bodily activity is caused by neurological changes in the central nervous system. The mind is part of the body. How changes in sense organs affect it, and how changes in it affect the muscles, become a painstaking matter of detailed scientific research which has no insoluble mystery attached to it.

But human mental life also embraces awareness by phenomenal properties. Such awareness is also, we must suppose, caused by changes in sense organs and brain. How this is done we do not know. Because the non-material seems to thwart our attempts to account for its operations, I suspect we will never know how the trick is worked. This part of the Mind-Body problem seems insoluble. This aspect of humanity seems destined to remain forever beyond our understanding.

So we reach a skeptical conclusion regarding one facet of the Mind-Body problem. Philosophers ought to dislike skeptical conclusions, but they should not like spurious escapes from them any better. We cannot guarantee in advance that the whole of human nature is open to human comprehension.

The new Epiphenomenalism denies, in its own way, three of the four incompatible propositions which set up the Mind-Body problem. The theory affirms that although only physical causes act on the human body, and all its physicochemical processes proceed in accordance with physical law, some processes occur in it which are not of a material kind. To that extent the body is not a purely material thing.

But it is also most misleading to say that on this theory the mind is a spiritual thing. The mind is the brain, and insofar as the mind is a cause, it is a physical cause of behavior. The mind cannot exist independently of the body or survive that body's dissolution. A man whose brain is destroyed is *ipso facto* a man who has lost his mind. Nevertheless some mental processes are, as we use the term, spiritual.

The third proposition, that *mind* and body interact, is accepted without qualification in the new Epiphenomenalism. The fourth, that matter and *spirit* do not interact, involves two sorts of processes, the action of the material on the spiritual, and the action of spirit on matter. The latter is denied in this theory, although the former is affirmed. Some material processes have non-material effects, but the converse never holds. The new Epiphenomenalism rejects only one half of the inter-action of matter and spirit.

This being so, one who holds to the theory must just grit his teeth and assert that a fundamental, anom-alous, causal connection relates some bodily processes to some non-material processes. He must insist that this is a brute fact we must learn to live with, however in-convenient it might be for our tidy world-schemes.

(iv) The Problem of Other Minds

The problem of Other Minds is the problem of how, if at all, we can know about the minds of other people. It is a problem because we can learn of others only by perceiving their bodies and the effects of their bodily actions, and we feel that there is a gulf to be bridged in knowing, from overt bodily activity, about the covert mind behind it. We reflect that what seem to be other people might be mindless automata, or beings who look and act like men but have minds quite different from ours, or even beings very like men except that they are spectacularly successful deceivers. It is not at all easy to satisfactorily dismiss the doubt about our knowledge of the minds of others which these reflec-tions raise.

The Behaviorists deny that there is any real prob-lem. They deny that the mind is in any sense some-thing inner behind behavior, and hence they deny that there is any exceptionally doubtful step from behavior to mind. But the problem will not disappear so readily;

that is another way of expressing the unsatisfactorily "outer" emphasis of Behaviorism.

Central-State Materialists construe the problem of Other Minds as a problem in establishing like causes for like behavioral effects. This is more difficult than the task the Behaviorists set themselves, which is merely that of establishing what everyone admits, that men, for all their differences, behave in strikingly similar ways. Nevertheless, the Central-State Materialist's problem is manageable within a reasonable view of the kinds of knowledge men can have. It is a problem in scientific theorizing. We must speculate on whether the inner causes of behavior in others are the same as those in ourselves. The evidence for a common physiology in all men is tremendous, and the direct investigations of nervous function in men point to the conclusion that the causes of behavior are alike in all men. In Central-State Materialism the problem of Other Minds is just like the "problem of other quasars" which asks: Do all quasars have a like constitution, and do they all operate on the same principles? And more thorough investigation of quasars, like more thorough investigation of men, will give us a more and more solid answer.

For the new Epiphenomenalism, however, the problem of Other Minds is more complex. It divides, like the Mind-Body problem, into a soluble and an insoluble part. In its soluble part, it treats the problem exactly like materialism does. Can we know another man has a mind? Yes, we can establish, as a well-grounded hypothesis, that his behavior has inner causes describable in psychological terms. Can we know that he is angry? Yes, we can establish that in him is a cause of gnashing, shouting, and hostility. And by showing that in both of us the causes of behavior lie in the brain, we show both that he has a mind, as we do, and that he has a mind like ours. Can we know another can see? Yes, by studying his powers of discrimination. Can we know he has color vision? Yes, in the same way. Can we know he is color blind? Yes, by finding diminished powers of discrimination. But what of how phenomenal properties seem to him? Can we know he sees colors or feels burns as we do? No, we cannot. If he is different in this respect, it is not a difference which will show in his behavior. Nor can the question be settled by finding his brain-states exactly parallel ours in their physicochemical properties. Other men may be imitation men.

Whether things seem to us as they do to him remains hidden behind the words which we both use to describe our experience. Even if he feels crushed when we feel burned, he will describe his feeling as a burning pain—the kind typically produced by burns, just as we do. Perhaps an imitation man, who has no sensations at all, might betray himself by failing to understand our attempts at phenomenal description, but an imitation man with a sufficient richness of spontaneous belief would, I think, remain undetected.

According to the new Epiphenomenalism, the minds of men are partly disclosed and partly hidden from one another. In much of central importance, the minds of others are open to our investigation. Yet in some aspects they remain mysterious. As I think this accurately states our situation with regard to our fellows, I count this consequence a confirmation of the new Epiphenomenalism.

(v) The Problems of Evolution and Embryonic Development

In discussing the difficulties of Dualism, we pointed out that anyone who held that the mind is a separable, spiritual thing must face the daunting tasks of identifying the point at which such a thing first appears. Where, in the apparently continuous sequence of forms beginning with protein molecules and ending with man, does spirit first enter? Why at that point rather than earlier or later in the sequence? How is spirit brought into being? Parallel questions arise for the development of the individual person from a fertilized ovum.

Similar difficulties, equally embarrassing, face the new Epiphenomenalism. If, among the properties of the brain, are some which are not purely physicochemical, at what point, and how, do such properties first make their appearance? Because the awareness of phenomenal properties is an essentially mental affair, it would seem reasonable to guess that it exists, primitively no doubt, where mind, as cause of behavior, is first present. Just what point that is, is an ambiguous matter. The most precise answer we seem likely to get is: where there is a central nervous system there is a mind.

We are then faced with two choices. We can hold that all matter, however organized, has properties other than physicochemical ones, but that only in nervous organization do they show themselves or "come to the surface," as it were. This view is panpsychism, the doctrine that no matter can be completely described in physical terms alone.

In chapter 2 we said that this alternative extends the field of the mental beyond the area in which there is direct evidence for it, and we must now go a little further into the question. Panpsychism likens awareness by phenomenal properties to, for example, the establishment of a "magnetic bottle", a magnetic field with a definite shape for containing charged elementary particles. A magnetic bottle can only be created by a particular complex organization of matter, yet its establishment depends upon the existence, in unorganized matter, not of shaped fields but of other properties which in a suitable arrangement cooperate to form a shaped magnetic field. Although only complexes can form magnetic bottles, the shaped field is not an evolutionary novelty. It is. a consequence, in a complex situation, of properties that its simple parts have in any event.

The great difference between the novelty of shaped magnetic fields and the novelty of awareness by phenomenal properties is this: the properties of simple material particles which cooperate in forming the first can be investigated in isolation, quite apart from their appearance in forming magnetic bottles. But properties cooperating in phenomenal awareness are accessible only in the complex manifestation. So the cooperating properties of matter in the unorganized state which panpsychism postulates are doomed to be forever beyond the reach of proper research. Consequently, panpsychism will never be able to explain how these quite unknown extra properties of particles and atoms combine to yield awareness by phenomenal properties. It promises an explanation but can never produce it.

In the light of these reflections the second alternative open to the new Epiphenomenalism seems more honest and more economical. This is the doctrine of real novelty. Let us label the doctrine *Emergence*. Emergence theory maintains that the appearance of non-physical properties in neural systems is not a co-operative effect of properties of their simpler parts. It is a quite new phenomenon, which just emerges in a certain sort of physical system. There is not, and cannot be, any explanation for such a fact. If it is a fact, it is a brute fact. Theorists do not like brute facts, but the panpsychist alternative merely camouflages their brutality without really removing it.

These two choices are the only ones available. The notion that awareness by phenomenal properties can be explained, like the magnetic bottle, by appeal to cooperating properties we already know about, is the doctrine of Central-State Materialism which has already been rejected. The idea that in unorganized matter, explaining properties are to be found not among those already recognized but in some as yet undiscovered, is the idea of an unspecified neo-materialism which must be ignored until it is specified.

Epiphenomenalists must just accept, if they are to remain Epiphenomenalists, that the existence of non-material properties is a fact for which they have no explanation. They may comfort themselves in this uncomfortable position with two reflections: the lack of explanation does not disprove the fact, and the existence of basic *material* properties of material things is something for which we equally have no explanation.

Compared with Epiphenomenalism, Central-State Materialism embodies a single, simple, and universal vision of the world. But we should not be prepared to pay for tidiness of theory the price of denying some of the facts. Epiphenomenalism rests on the claim that not all facts about men's minds will fit into the materialist account. If that claim is correct, we will have to reconcile ourselves to an interpretation of evolutionary theory and embryonic development which is less smooth and unproblematic than we might wish.

(vi) The Current State of the Mind-Body Problem

In some ways, any decision on the Mind-Body problem reached at the moment would be premature. We just do not know enough about ourselves to be sure what the relation of mind to body must be. This has already emerged in several parts of the discussion. The unchallengeable establishment of the reality of paranormal phenomena would demolish both Central-State Materialism and the new Epiphenomenalism. And we cannot yet say with a clear mind either that this has been or will be established, nor that it will not.

Again, the discovery of brain activity, connected with mental activity, yet violating the laws of physics and chemistry, would demolish both Materialism and Epiphenomenalism. And no one can say such a discovery will never be made.

On both these fronts, we are hampered by the inadequacies of our empirical knowledge. And on the other hand, our philosophical development is insufficiently advanced. It is not yet clear whether our awareness by phenomenal properties is compatible with Materialism. Nor whether the sort of freedom we know we have is compatible with anything but Dualism. Nor whether the intentionality of mental states can afford any clue to the nature of mind. Nor even whether the assumptions involved in the way the Mind-Body problem is formulated do not fatally distort the whole question.

These uncertainties make it premature to regard the Mind-Body question as closed. This will probably be the case so long as there are men to think. But to embrace some view of the Mind-Body question as a working hypothesis is never premature. We need some view of our own nature, even if it is provisional.

Because Central-State Materialism represents the simplest, least compromising view of the matter, the ways in which it is vulnerable should command our attention in attempting to make progress with the Mind-Body problem. We can learn most by examining whether, and for what reason, mental objects such as images and dreams, mental processes such as enduring a stinging pain, mental descriptions with their intentionality, resist being brought within the fold of Materialism. These questions are not yet settled. Philosophy is not yet complete.

BIBLIOGRAPHY

Works have been classified in this bibliography according to their predominant theme, but many naturally discuss matters covered by other classifications. The articles grouped under a heading include both defenses of, and attacks upon, the topic in question and readers following up a topic are urged to read examples of both.

The bibliography aims at being reasonably comprehensive in the recent discussions of the Mind-Body problem itself, but to avoid lists of unmanageable size much ancillary literature is omitted. The reader should realize that the list is selective, sketchy, and deficient on the topics: *Privacy and Introspection, Other Minds, Parapsychology, Intentionality, Minds and Machines, Immortality,* and the doctrines of *Strawson* and *Wittgenstein,* not to mention *Freedom, Action and Passion,* etc. The philosophy of mind is a subject broader than the Mind-Body problem.

In using the bibliography, readers are advised to look rapidly over several of the items listed, then settle down to serious study of those which seem best to meet their needs.

The following abbreviations have been used:

AJP	*The Australasian Journal of Philosophy*
APQ	*American Philosophical Quarterly*
BJPS	*The British Journal for Philosophy of Science*
J. Phil	*The Journal of Philosophy*
PAS	*Proceedings of the Aristotelian Society*
Phil. and Phenom. Research	*Philosophy and Phenomenological Research*
Phil. Quarterly	*The Philosophical Quarterly*
Phil. Review	*The Philosophical Review*
Phil. Studies	*Philosophical Studies*
Phil. Topics	*Philosophical Topics*
Rev. Metaphysics	*The Review of Metaphysics*

References to journal articles are made as follows:
Name of journal, volume number, volume year, pages. For example, "*J. Phil* 66 (1969) 97–112," is the abbreviation of "*The Journal of Philosophy*, volume 66 (1969), pages 97–112."

GENERAL DISCUSSIONS OF THE PROBLEM

BOOKS

An immensely useful reference work, containing discussions of all the issues raised in this book, is:

Edwards, Paul, ed. *The Encyclopedia of Philosophy,* 8 vols. New York, 1967.

OTHER GENERAL WORKS

Aristotle, *De Anima.*
Bain, Alexander. *Mind and Body.* London, 1973.
Broad, C. D. *The Mind and Its Place in Nature.* London, 1925.
Drake, Durant. *Mind and Its Place in Nature.* New York, 1925.
Krikorian, Y. H., ed. *Naturalism and the Human Mind.* New York, 1944.
Kneale, William. *On Having a Mind.* Cambridge, 1962.
Laird, John. *Our Minds and Their Bodies.* London, 1925.
Passmore, John. *A Hundred Years of Philosophy.* London, 1925. Second ed., 1966.
Peursen, C. A. van. *Body, Soul, Spirit: A Survey of the Body-Mind Problem.* Oxford, 1966.
Pratt, J. B. *Matter and Spirit.* New York, 1926.
Reeves, John Wynn. *Body and Mind in Western Thought.* Harmondsworth, 1958.
Stout, G. F. *Mind and Matter.* Cambridge, 1931.
Vesey, G. N. A. *The Embodied Mind.* London, 1965.

INTRODUCTORY TEXTS

Churchland, P. M. *Matter and Consciousness: A Contemporary Introduction to the Philosophy of Mind.* Chicago, 1983.

Shaffer, Jerome A. *Philosophy of Mind.* Englewood Cliffs, N.J., 1968.

Taylor, Richard. *Metaphysics.* Englewood Cliffs, N.J., 1964.

White, Alan R. *The Philosophy of Mind.* New York, 1967.

Wisdom, John. *Problems of Mind and Matter.* Cambridge, 1934. Paperback. 1963.

ARTICLES

Armstrong, D. M., "Recent Work on the Relation of Mind and Brain," in *Contemporary Philosophy,* vol. 4, pp. 45–79, The Hague, 1983.

Beck, L. W., "The Psychophysical as a Pseudo-Problem," *J. Phil* 37 (1940) 561–571.

Hardie, W. F. R., "Aristotle's Treatment of the Relation between the Soul and the Body," *Phil. Quarterly* 14 (1964) 53–72.

Kneale, Martha, "What is the Mind-Body Problem?" *PAS* 50 (1949–50) 105–122.

Mace, C. A., "The 'Body-Mind Problem' in Philosophy, Psychology, and Medicine," *Philosophy* 41 (1966) 153–164.

———, "Some Trends in the Philosophy of Mind," in *British Philosophy in Mid-Century,* ed. C. A. Mace, London, 1957.

Miles, T. R., "The 'Mental'-'Physical' Dichotomy," *PAS* (1963–64) 71–84.

Popper, K. R., "Language and the Body-Mind Problem," *Proceedings of the 11th International Congress of Philosophy* 7 (1953) 101–107.

Puccetti, Roland, "Science, Analysis, and the Problem of Mind," *Philosophy* 39 (1964) 249-259.

Sellars, W. S., "Aristotelian Philosophies of Mind," in *Philosophy for the Future,* eds. R. W. Sellars, V. J. McGill, and Marvin Farber, New York, 1949.

Shaffer, Jerome A., "Recent Work on the Mind-Body Problem," *APQ* 2 (1965) 81-104.

Watanabe, Satosi, "A Model of Mind-Body Relations in Terms of Modular Logic," in *Boston Studies in the Philosophy of Science: Proceedings of the Boston Colloquium of the Philosophy of Science, 1961/ 1962,* ed. M. W. Wartofsky, Dordrecht, 1962.

Weber, C. O., "Theoretical and Experimental Difficulties of Modern Psychology with the Mind-Body Problem" in *Twentieth Century Psychology,* ed. P. L. Harriman, New York, 1946.

Whiteley, C. H., "The Relation between Mind and Body," *PAS* 45 (1944-45) 119-129.

Wisdom, J. O., "A New Model for the Mind-Body Relationship," *BJPS* 2 (1951-52) 295-301.

DUALISM

BOOKS

Balz, A. G. A. *Cartesian Studies.* New York, 1951.

Beloff, John. *The Existence of Mind.* London, 1962.

Bergson, Henri. *Matter and Memory,* trs. W. M. Paul and W. Scott Palmer. London, 1908.

Campbell, C. A. *On Selfhood and Godhood.* London, 1957.

Descartes, René. *Meditations* and *Passions of the Soul,* in *The Philosophical Works of Descartes,* tr. E. S. Haldane and G. R. T. Ross. Cambridge, 1911.

Driesch, H. A. E. *Mind and Body: A Criticism of Psychophysical Parallelism,* tr. Theodore Besterman. London, 1927.

Ducasse, C. J. *A Critical Examination of the Belief in a Life after Death.* Springfield, Ill., 1961.

———. *Nature, Mind and Death.* La Salle, Ill., 1951.

Eccles, J. C. *The Neurophysiological Basis of Mind.* Oxford, 1953.

Jackson, F. C. *Perception.* Cambridge, 1977.

Kapp, R. O. *Mind, Life and Body.* London, 1951.

Leibniz, Gottfried. *Exposition and Defence of the New System,* in his *Philosophical Writings,* sel. and tr. Mary Morris. London, 1934.

Lotze, I. *Microcosmus,* in his *Collected Works,* Vol. 1. Edinburgh, 1885.

Maher, Michael. *Psychology.* London, 1940.

Malebranche, Nicolas. *Dialogues on Metaphysics and on Religion,* tr. Morris Ginsberg. London, 1923.

McDougall, William. *Body and Mind: A History and Defence of Animism.* London, 1911.

Popper, K. R., and J. C. Eccles. *The Self and Its Brain.* New York, 1977.

Vendler, Z. *Res Cogitans.* Cornell, 1972.

ARTICLES

Ballard, E. G., "Descartes' Revision of the Cartesian Dualism," *Phil. Quarterly* 7 (1957) 249–259.

Ewing, A. C., "Are Mental Attributes Attributes of the Body?" *PAS* 45 (1944–45) 27–58.

Freed, Lan, "Dualism and Language," *BJPS* 3 (1952–53) 327–338.

Golightly, Cornelius L., "Mind-Body, Causation and Correlation," *Philosophy of Science* 19 (1952) 225–227.

Landesman, Charles, "The New Dualism in the Philosophy of Mind," *Rev. Metaphysics* 19 (1965) 329–345.

Long, D., "Disembodied Existence, Physicalism, and the Mind-Body Problem," *Phil. Studies* 31 (1977) 307–316.

Luce, D. R., "The Action of Mind on Body," *Philosophy of Science* 27 (1960) 171–182.

Quinton, A. M., "The Soul," *J. Phil* 59 (1962) 393–409.

Roelofs, Howard D., "A Case for Dualism and Interaction," *Phil. and Phenom. Research* 15 (1955) 451–476.

_____, "Second Thoughts on Causation, Dualism and Interaction," *Mind* 56 (1947) 60–71.

Swinburne, R., "Are Mental Events Identical with Brain Events?" *APQ* 19 (1982) 173–181.

BEHAVIORISM

Discussions whose primary inspiration is from science:

BOOKS

Hull, C. L. *Principles of Behavior.* New York, 1943.

Singer, E. A. *Mind as Behavior.* Columbus, Ohio, 1924.

Skinner, B. F. *Science and Human Behavior.* New York, 1953.

_____, *Verbal Behavior.* New York, 1957.

Taylor, James G. *The Behavioral Basis of Perception.* New Haven, Conn., 1962.

Watson, J. B. *Behaviorism.* New York, 1924.

ARTICLES

Chomsky, Noam, "A Review of B. F. Skinner's *Verbal Behaviour,*" *Language* 35 (1959) 26–58.

Farrell, B. A., "Critical Notice of James G. Taylor, *The Behavioral Basis of Perception,*" *Mind* 74 (1965) 259–280.

Hunter, W. S., "The Problem of Consciousness," *Psychological Review* 31 (1924) 1–31.

Lashley, K. S., "The Behaviouristic Interpretation of Consciousness," *Psychological Review* 30 (1923) 237–272, 329–353.

McGill, V. J., and Livingston Welch, "A Behaviourist Analysis of Emotions," *Philosophy of Science* 13 (1946) 100–122.

O'Neil, W. M., "The Relation of Inner Experience and Overt Behaviour," *AJP* 27 (1949) 27–45.

Skinner, B. F., "The Operational Analysis of Psychological Terms," *Psychological Review* 52 (1945) 270–277, also in *Readings in the Philosophy of Science,* eds. Herbert Feigl and May Brodbeck, New York, 1953.

Spence, Kenneth W., "The Empirical Basis and Theoretical Structure of Psychology," *Philosophy of Science* 24 (1957) 97–108.

Stephenson, William, "Postulates of Behaviourism." *Philosophy of Science* 20 (1953) 110–120.

Taylor, J. G., "Towards a Science of Mind," *Mind* 66 (1957) 434–452.

Tolman, E. C., "A Behaviourist's Definition of Consciousness," *Psychological Review* 34 (1927) 433–439.

————, "Operational Behaviourism and Current Trends in Psychology," in *Proceedings of the 25th Anniversary Celebration of the Inauguration of Graduate Studies,* University of Southern California, Los Angeles, 1936.

Discussions in which philosophical considerations are paramount:

BOOKS

Hampshire, Stuart. *Feeling and Expression.* London, 1961.

Malcolm, Norman. *Dreaming.* London, 1959.

Melden, A. I. *Free Action.* London, 1961.

Ryle, Gilbert. *The Concept of Mind.* London, 1949.

Taylor, Charles. *The Explanation of Behavior.* New York, 1964.

Wisdom, John. *Other Minds.* Oxford, 1952.

Wittgenstein, Ludwig. *Philosophical Investigations.* London, 1953.

ARTICLES

Aaron, R. I., "Dispensing with Mind," *PAS* 52 (1951-52) 225-242.

Aldrich, Virgil G., "Behavior, Simulating and Non-Simulating," *J. Phil* 63 (1966) 453-457.

Allen, A. H. B., "Other Minds," *Mind* 61 (1952) 328-348.

Aune, Bruce, "On Thought and Feeling," *Phil. Quarterly* 13 (1963) 1-12.

Blanshard, Brand, and B. F. Skinner, "The Problem of Consciousness—A Debate," *Phil. and Phenom. Research* 27 (1966-67) 317-337.

Block, N. J., "Psychologism and Behaviorism," *Phil. Review* 90 (1981) 5-43.

Campbell, C. A., "Ryle on the Intellect," *Phil. Quarterly* 3 (1953) 115-138, and in his *In Defense of Free Will,* New York, 1967.

Carnap, Rudolf, "Logical Foundations of the Unity of Science," in *Readings in Philosophical Analysis,* eds. Herbert Feigl and W. S. Sellars, New York, 1949.

———, "Psychology in Physical Language," in *Logical Positivism,* ed. A. J. Ayer, Glencoe, Ill., 1959.

———, "Testability and Meaning," *Philosophy of Science* 3 (1936) 419-471, 4 (1937) 1-40, also in *Readings in the Philosophy of Science,* eds. Feigl and Brodbeck.

Dewan, Edmond M., " 'Other Minds': An Application of Recent Epistemological Ideas to the Definition of Consciousness," *Philosophy of Science* 24 (1957) 70-76.

Dobbs, H. A. C., " 'Substance' in Psychology," *Mind* 55 (1946) 193-203.

Ewing, A. C., "Mental Acts," *Mind* 57 (1948) 201-220.

———, "Professor Ryle's Attack on Dualism," *PAS* 53 (1952-53) 47-48, also in *Clarity Is Not Enough,* ed. H. D. Lewis, London, 1963.

Farrell, B. A., "Experience," *Mind* 59 (1950) 170-198.

Feigl, Herbert, "The Mind-Body Problem in the Development of Logical Empiricism," *Revue Internationale de Philosophie* 4 (1950) 64–83, also in *Readings in the Philosophy of Science*, eds. Feigl and Brodbeck.

———, "Physicalism, Unity of Science and the Foundations of Psychology," in *The Philosophy of Rudolf Carnap*, ed. P. A. Schilpp, La Salle, Ill., 1963.

Findlay, J. N., "Linguistic Approach to Psycho-physics," *PAS* 50 (1949–50) 43–64.

———, "On Mind and Our Knowledge of It," *Philosophy* 20 (1945) 206–226.

Garnet, A. Campbell, "Mind as Minding," *Mind* 61 (1952) 349–358.

Ginnane, W. J., "Thoughts," *Mind* 69 (1960) 372–390.

Hamlyn, D. W., "Behaviour," *Philosophy* 28 (1953) 132–145.

Hampshire, Stuart, "The Analogy of Feeling," *Mind* 61 (1952) 1–12.

Hempel, Carl G., "The Logical Analysis of Psychology," tr. W. S. Sellars, in *Readings in Philosophical Analysis*, eds. Feigl and Sellars.

Joske, W. D., "Behaviourism as a Scientific Theory," *Phil. and Phenom. Research* 22 (1961–62) 61–68.

King, Hugh R., "Professor Ryle and *The Concept of Mind*," *J. Phil* 48 (1951) 280–296.

Krikorian, Y. H., "The Publicity of Mind," *Phil. and Phenom. Research* 22 (1961–62) 317–325.

Lewis, C. I., "Some Logical Considerations Concerning the Mental," in *Readings in Philosophical Analysis*, eds. Feigl and Sellars.

Lucas, J. R., "The Soul," in *Faith and Logic*, ed. Basil Mitchell, London, 1957.

McCloskey, Mary, "Minds," *AJP* 40 (1962) 303–312.

McCormick, Suzanne and Irving Thalberg, "Trying," *Dialogue* 61 (1967) 29–46.

MacDonald, Margaret, "Professor Ryle on the Concept of Mind," *Phil. Review* 60 (1951) 80–90.

Malcolm, Norman, "Behaviorism as a Philosophy of

Psychology," in *Behaviorism and Phenomenology,* ed. T. W. Wann, Chicago, 1964.

Miller, D. S., "'Descartes' Myth' and Professor Ryle's Fallacy," *J. Phil* 48 (1951) 270–280.

Mundle, C. W. K., "Mental Concepts," *Mind* 72 (1963) 577–580.

Pap, Arthur, "Semantic Analysis and Psycho-Physical Dualism," *Mind* 61 (1952) 209–221.

Pears, D. F., "Professor Norman Malcolm: *Dreaming,"* *Mind* 70 (1961) 145–163.

Price, H. H., "Some Objections to Behaviorism," in *Dimensions of Mind,* ed. Sidney Hook, New York, 1961.

Putnam, Hilary, "Brains and Behaviour," in *Analytical Philosophy,* ed. R. J. Butler, Second Series, Oxford, 1965.

———, "Dreaming and 'Depth Grammar,'" in *Analytical Philosophy,* ed. R. J. Butler, Oxford, 1962.

———, "Psychological Concepts, Explication, and Ordinary Language," *J. Phil* 54 (1957) 94–100.

Quine, W. V., "On Mental Entities," *Proceedings of the American Academy of Arts and Sciences* 80 (1950), and in his *Ways of Paradox,* New York, 1967.

Ruddick, William, "On Responses and Reactions," *AJP* 46 (1968) 65–78.

Ryle, Gilbert, "Feelings," *Phil. Quarterly* 1 (1951) 193–205.

———, "Sensation," in *Contemporary British Philosophy,* Third Series, ed. H. D. Lewis, London, 1956.

Scriven, Michael, "A Study of Radical Behaviorism," in *Foundations of Science and the Concepts of Psychology and Psychoanalysis,* eds. Herbert Feigl and Michael Scriven, Minnesota Studies in the Philosophy of Science, vol. 1, Minneapolis, 1956.

Sellars, W. S., "Mind, Meaning, and Behavior," *Phil. Studies* 3 (1952) 83–94.

Sibley, Frank, "A Theory of the Mind," *Rev. Metaphysics* 4 (1950–51) 259–278.

Smart, J. J. C., "Ryle on Mechanism and Psychology," *Phil. Quarterly* 9 (1959) 349-355.

Weitz, Morris, "Professor Ryle's 'Logical Behaviourism,'" *J. Phil* 48 (1951) 297-301.

Whiteley, C. H., "Behaviourism," *Mind* 70 (1961) 164-174.

Wisdom, John, "The Concept of Mind," *PAS* 50 (1949-50) 189-204.

Wright, J. N., "Mind and *The Concept of Mind,*" *PAS*, Supp. Vol. 33 (1959) 1-22.

Ziff, Paul, "About Behaviourism," *Analysis* 18 (1958) 132-136.

MATERIALISM

Central State Materialism and the Causal Theory of Mind:

BOOKS

Adrian, E. D. *The Mechanism of Nervous Action.* Philadelphia, 1932.

_____. *The Physical Background of Perception.* Oxford, 1947.

Armstrong, D. M. *Bodily Sensations.* London, 1962.

_____. *A Materialist Theory of the Mind.* London, 1968.

_____. *The Nature of Mind and Other Essays.* Cornell, 1981.

Ashby, W. R. *Design for a Brain.* New York, 1952.

Boring, E. G. *The Physical Dimensions of Consciousness.* New York, 1933.

Brain, W. R. *The Physical Basis of Mind.* Oxford, 1950.

Eliot, Hugh. *Modern Science and Materialism.* London, 1919.

Feigl, Herbert. *The "Mental" and the "Physical": The Essay and a Postscript.* Minneapolis, 1967.

Hayek, F. A. *The Sensory Order.* London, 1952.

Hebb, D. O. *The Organization of Behavior.* New York, 1949.

Hobbes, Thomas. *De corpore* (excerpts in R. S. Peters' edition of Hobbes entitled *Body, Man, and Citizen,* New York, 1962).

Lange, F. A. *A History of Materialism,* tr. E. C. Thomas. London, 1925.

Laslett, Peter, ed. *The Physical Basis of Mind.* Oxford, 1951.

Lucretius. *De rerum natura. (On the Nature of the Universe,* tr. Ronald Latham. Harmondsworth, 1951.)

Presley, C. F., ed. *The Identity Theory of Mind.* Brisbane, 1967.

Smart, J. J. C. *Philosophy and Scientific Realism.* London, 1963.

Wilkes, K. V. *Physicalism.* London, 1978.

ARTICLES

Ashby, W. R., "The Nervous System as Physical Machine," *Mind* 56 (1947) 44–59.

Baier, Kurt, "Pains," *AJP* 40 (1962) 1–23.

———, "Smart on Sensations," *AJP* 40 (1962) 57–68.

Black, Max, "Some Questions about Materialism," *Phil. Review* 55 (1946) 572–579.

Boring, E. G., "Mind and Mechanism," *American Journal of Psychology* 59 (1946) 173–192.

Bradley, M. C., "Sensations, Brain-Processes, and Colours," *AJP* 41 (1963) 385–393.

———, "Two Arguments Against the Identity Thesis," in *Contemporary Philosophy in Australia,* eds. R. Brown and C. D. Rollins, London, 1969.

Brandt, Richard, and Jaegwon Kim, "The Logic of the Identity Theory," *J. Phil* 64 (1967) 515–537.

Campbell, Keith, "Critical Notice of *The Identity Theory of Mind,* ed. C. F. Presley," *AJP* 46 (1968) 175–188.

Cohen, Henry, "The Status of Brain in the Concept of Mind," *Philosophy* 27 (1952) 195–210.

Cornman, James W., "The Identity of Mind and Body," *J. Phil* 59 (1962) 486–492.

Earman, J., "What Is Physicalism?" *J. Phil* 72 (1975) 565–567.

Ellis, Brian, "Physical Monism," *Synthese* 17 (1967) 141–161.

Enc, B., "In Defense of the Identity Theory," *J. Phil* 80 (1983) 279–298.

Feigl, Herbert, "The 'Mental' and the 'Physical,'" in *Concepts, Theories, and the Mind-Body Problem,* eds. Herbert Feigl, Michael Scriven, and Grover Maxwell, Minnesota Studies in the Philosophy of Science, vol. 2, Minneapolis, 1958.

Feyerabend, P. K., "Materialism and the Mind-Body Problem," *Rev. Metaphysics* 17 (1963–64) 49–66.

———, "Mental Events and the Brain," *J. Phil* 68 (1963) 295–296.

Garnett, A. Campbell, "Body and Mind—The Identity Thesis," *AJP* 43 (1965) 77–81; with reply by J. J. C. Smart.

Goldman, Alvin I., "A Causal Theory of Knowing," *J. Phil* 64 (1967) 357–372.

Grice, H. P., "The Causal Theory of Perception," *PAS,* Supp. vol. 35 (1961) 121–152.

Gustafson, Don F., "On the Identity Theory," *Analysis* 24 (1963) 30–32.

Hochberg, Herbert, "Physicalism, Behaviourism, and Phenomena," *Philosophy of Science* 26 (1959) 93–103.

Hocutt, Max, "In Defense of Materialism," *Phil. and Phenom. Research* 27 (1966–67) 366–385.

Hoffman, Robert, "Malcolm and Smart on Brain-Mind Identity," *Philosophy* 42 (1967) 128–136.

Kekes, John, "Physicalism, the Identity Theory, and the Doctrine of Emergence," *Philosophy of Science* 33 (1966) 360–375.

Kim, Jaegwon, "On the Psycho-Physical Identity Theory," *APQ* 3 (1966) 277–285.

———, "Phenomenal Properties, Psychological Laws, and the Identity Theory," *Monist* 56 (1972) 177–192.

Kitcher, P., "Phenomenal Qualities," *APQ* 16 (1979) 123–129.

Kotarbinski, T., "The Fundamental Ideas of Pansomatism," *Mind* 64 (1955) 488–500.

Lewis, David K., "An Argument for the Identity Theory," *J. Phil* 63 (1966) 17–25.

———, "Psychophysical and Theoretical Identifications," *AJP* 50 (1972) 249–258.

Malcolm, Norman, "The Conceivability of Mechanism," *Phil. Review* 77 (1968) 45–72.

———, "Scientific Materialism and the Identity Theory," *Dialogue* 3 (1964–65) 115–125.

Maxwell, Nicholas, "Understanding Sensations," *AJP* 46 (1968) 127–145.

Medlin, Brian, "Materialism and the Argument from Distinct Existences," in *The Business of Reason*, eds. J. J. MacIntosh and S. C. Coval, London, 1969.

———, "Ryle and the Mechanical Hypothesis," in *The Identity Theory of Mind*, ed. Presley.

Meehl, Paul, "The Compleat Autocerebroscopist," in *Mind, Matter, and Method*, eds. P. K. Feyerabend and G. E. Maxwell, Minneapolis, 1966.

Nagel, Thomas, "Physicalism," *Phil. Review* 74 (1965) 339–356.

———, "What Is It Like to Be a Bat?" *Phil. Review* 83 (1974) 435–450.

Pappas, G., "Armstrong's Materialism," *Canadian Journal of Philosophy* 7 (1977) 569–592.

Pitcher, George, "Sensations and Brain Processes: A Reply to Prof. Smart," *AJP* 38 (1960) 150–157.

Place, U. T., "Is Consciousness a Brain Process?" *British Journal of Psychology* 47 (1956) 44–50.

Raab, F. V., "Of Minds and Molecules," *Philosophy of Science* 32 (1965) 57–72.

Rorty, Richard, "Mind-Body Identity, Privacy, and Categories," *Rev. Metaphysics* 19 (1965) 24–54.

Routley, Richard, and Valerie Macrae, "On the Identity of Sensations and Physiological Occurrences," *APQ* 3 (1966) 87–110.

Scriven, Michael, "The Limitations of the Identity Theory," in *Mind, Matter, and Method,* eds. Feyerabend and Maxwell.

———, "The Mechanical Concept of Mind," *Mind* 62 (1953) 230–240.

Sellars, W. S., "The Identity Approach to the Mind-Body Problem," *Rev. Metaphysics* 18 (1965) 430–451.

Shaffer, Jerome A., "Could Mental States be Brain Processes?" *J. Phil* 58 (1961) 813–822.

———, "Mental Events and the Brain," *J. Phil* 60 (1963) 160–166.

Smart, J. J. C., "Brain Processes and Incorrigibility—A Reply to Prof. Baier," *AJP* 40 (1962) 68–70.

———, "Further Remarks on Sensations and Brain Processes," *Phil. Review* 70 (1961) 406–407.

———, "Further Thoughts on the Identity Theory," *Monist* 56 (1972) 149–162.

———, "Materialism," *J. Phil* 60 (1963) 651–662.

———, "Sensations and Brain Processes," *Phil. Review* 68 (1959) 141–156.

Stevenson, J. T., "Sensations and Brain Processes: A Reply to J. J. C. Smart," *Phil. Review* 69 (1960) 505–510.

Taylor, Charles, "Mind-Body Identity, a Side Issue?" *Phil. Review* 76 (1967) 201–213.

Taylor, Richard, "Comments on a Mechanistic Conception of Purposefulness," *Philosophy of Science* 17 (1950) 310–317.

Tomberlin, James E., "About the Identity Theory," *AJP* 43 (1965) 295–299.

Weissman, David, "A Note on the Identity Thesis," *Mind* 74 (1965) 571–577.

Williams, Donald, "Mind as a Matter of Fact," *Rev. Metaphysics* 13 (1959–60) 203–225.

_____, "Naturalism and the Nature of Things," *Phil. Review* 53 (1944) 417–443.

The Questions of Mentality in Electonic and Physiological Machines

Dreyfus, H. L. *What Computers Can't Do.* Rev. ed. New York, 1979.

_____, "Why Computers Must Have Bodies in Order to Be Intelligent," *Rev. Metaphysics* 21 (1967) 13–32.

George, F. H., "Could Machines Be Made to Think?" *Philosophy* 31 (1956) 244–252.

Gunderson, Keith, "Descartes, La Mettrie, Language and Machines," *Philosophy* 39 (1964) 193–222.

_____, "Robots, Consciousness and Programmed Behaviour," *BJPS* 19 (1968) 109–122.

Kane, R. H. "Turing Machines and Mental Reports," *AJP* 44 (1966) 344–352.

Lacey, A. R., "Men and Robots," *Phil. Quarterly* 10 (1960) 61–72.

Mays, W., "Can Machines Think?" *Philosophy* 27 (1952) 148–162.

Puccetti, Roland, "Can Humans Think?" *Analysis* 26 (1966) 198–202.

Putnam, Hilary, "The Mental Life of Some Machines," in *Intentionality, Minds, and Perception,* ed. H. N. Castañeda, Detroit, 1966.

_____, "Minds and Machines," in *Dimensions of Mind,* ed. Hook.

_____, "Robots: Machines or Artifically Created Life?" *J. Phil* (1964) 668–691.

Scriven, Michael, "The Compleat Robot," in *Dimensions of Mind,* ed. Hook.

Shwayder, D. S., "Man and Mechanism," *AJP* 41 (1963) 2–11.

Sluckin, Wladyslaw, *Minds and Machines.* Rev. ed. Harmondsworth, 1960.

Turing, A. M., "Computing Machinery and Intelligence," *Mind* 59 (1950) 433–460.

FUNCTIONALISM

BOOKS

Block, N. J., ed. *Readings in Philosophy of Psychology.* Vol. 1. Harvard, 1979.
Churchland, P. M. *Scientific Realism and the Plasticity of Mind.* Cambridge, 1979.
Dennett, D. C. *Brainstorms.* Montgomery, 1978.
Fodor, J. A. *Psychological Explanation.* New York, 1968.
Harman, G. *Thought.* Princeton, 1973.

ARTICLES

Block, N. J., "Are Absent Qualia Impossible?" *Phil. Review* 89 (1980) 257–274.
———, "Troubles with Functionalism," in *Perceptions and Cognitions: Issues in the Foundations of Psychology,* ed. C. Wade Savage, Minnesota Studies in the Philosophy of Science, vol. 9, Minneapolis, 1978.
———, and J. A. Fodor, "What Psychological States Are Not," *Phil. Review* 81 (1972) 159–181.
Campbell, Keith, "Abstract Particulars and the Philosophy of Mind," *AJP* 61 (1983) 129–141.
Churchland, P. M., and P. S. Churchland, "Functionalism, Qualia, and Intentionality," *Phil. Topics* 12 (1981) 121–145.
Davis, L., "Functionalism and Absent Qualia," *Phil. Studies* 41 (1982) 231–249.
Dennett, D. C., "Current Issues in the Philosophy of Mind," *APQ* 15 (1978) 249–261.
Eshelman, L., "Functionalism, Sensations, and Materialism," *Canadian Journal of Philosophy* 7 (1977) 255–274.

Jackson, F., Pargetter, R., and E. W. Prior, "Functionalism and Type-Type Identity Theories," *Phil. Studies* 42 (1982) 209-223.

Kim, J., "Causality, Identity and Supervenience in the Mind-Body Problem," *Midwest Studies in Philosophy* 4 (1979) 31-49.

———, "Psychophysical Supervenience," *Phil. Studies* 41 (1982) 51-70.

———, "Psychophysical Supervenience as a Mind-Body Theory," *Cognition and Brain Theory* 5 (1982) 129-147.

Kraut, R., "Sensory States and Sensory Objects," *Nous* 16 (1982) 277-293.

Lewis, D. K., "Man Pain and Martian Pain," in *Readings in the Philosophy of Psychology*, ed. N. Block, Harvard, 1979.

Lycan, W. G., "Form, Function, and Feel," *J. Phil* 78 (1981) 24-50.

———, "Mental States and Putnam's Functionalist Hypothesis," *AJP* 52 (1974) 48-62.

———, "Psychological Laws," *Phil. Topics* 12 (1981) 9-38.

———, "Toward a Homuncular Theory of Believing," *Cognition and Brain Theory* 4 (1981) 139-159.

Nelson, R. J., "Mechanism, Functionalism, and the Identity Theory," *J. Phil* 63 (1976) 365-385.

Putnam, H., "Psychological Predicates," in *Art, Mind and Religion*, ed. Capitan and Merrill, Pittsburgh, 1967.

———, "Reductionism and the Nature of Psychology," *Cognition* 2 (1973) 131-146.

Shoemaker, S., "Absent Qualia Are Impossible—A Reply to Block," *Phil. Review* 90 (1981) 585-599.

———, "Functionalism and Qualia," *Phil. Studies* 27 (1975) 291-315.

———, "The Inverted Spectrum," *J. Phil* 79 (1982) 357-381.

———, "Some Varieties of Functionalism," *Phil. Topics* 12 (1981) 93-120.

DOUBLE ASPECT THEORY

BOOKS

Hirst, R. J. *The Problems of Perception.* London, 1959.

Lamettrie, J. O. *Man a Machine,* trans. G. C. Bussey. La Salle, Ill., 1943.

Priestley, Joseph. *Disquisitions Relating to Matter and Spirit.* London, 1777.

O'Shaunnessy, Brian. *The Will, A Dual Aspect Theory.* Cambridge, 1980.

ARTICLES

Aldrich, Virgil C., "An Aspect Theory of Mind," *Phil. and Phenom. Research* 26 (1965–66) 313–326.

Brody, Nathan, and Paul Oppenheim, "Application of Bohr's Principle of Complementarity to the Mind-Body Problem," *J. Phil* 66 (1969) 97–112.

Meehl, P. E., and W. S. Sellars, "The Concept of Emergence," in *Foundations of Science and the Concepts of Psychology and Psychoanalysis,* eds. Feigl and Scriven, Minnesota Studies in the Philosophy of Science, vol. 1.

Nagel, Ernest, "Are Naturalists Materialists?" *J. Phil* 42 (1945) 515–553, and in his *Logic Without Metaphysics,* Glencoe, Ill., 1957.

Taylor, Richard, "How to Bury the Mind-Body Problem," *APQ* 6 (1969) 136–143.

STRAWSON'S VIEW

Strawson, P. F. *Individuals.* London, 1959.

Aldrich, Virgil C., "Reflections on Ayer's *The Concept of a Person,*" *J. Phil* 62 (1965) 111–128.

Ayer, A. J., "The Concept of a Person," in his *Concept of a Person and Other Essays,* London, 1963.

Coburn, Robert C., "Persons and Psychological Concepts," *APQ* 4 (1967) 208–221.

Lewis, H. D., "Mind and Body—Some Observations on Mr. Strawson's Views," *PAS* 63 (1962–63) 1–22, and in *Clarity is Not Enough,* ed. H. D. Lewis, London, 1963.

Martin, C. B., "People," *Contemporary Philosophy in Australia,* eds. R. Brown and C. D. Rollins, London, 1969.

Pears, David, "Critical Study of P. F. Strawson, *Individuals,"* *Phil. Quarterly* 11 (1961) 172–185.

Puccetti, Roland, "Mr. Strawson's Concept of a Person," *AJP* 45 (1967) 321–328.

Rollins, C. D., "Personal Predicates," *Phil. Quarterly* 10 (1960) 1–11.

EPIPHENOMENALISM

Huxley, T. H., "On the Hypothesis that Minds are Automata and its History," in his *Methods and Results,* London, 1894.

Jackson, F. C., "Epiphenomenal Qualia," *Phil. Quarterly* 32 (1982) 127–136.

———, Review of Campbell, K., *Body and Mind, AJP* 50 (1972) 77–80.

Kneale, William, "Broad on Mental Events and Epiphenomenalism," in *The Philosophy of C. D. Broad,* ed. P. A. Schilpp, New York, 1959.

Lachs, John, "Epiphenomenalism and the Notion of Cause," *J. Phil* 60 (1963) 141–145.

———, "The Impotent Mind," *Rev. Metaphysics* 17 (1963–64) 187–199.

Santayana, George. *Reason and Common Sense.* New York, 1922. Paperback 1962.

Watson, George, "Apparent Motion and the Mind-Body Problem," *BJPS* 2 (1951–52) 236–247.

Woodhouse, M., "A New Epiphenomenalism?" *AJP* 52 (1974) 163–169, with comments by Keith Campbell following.

INTENTIONALITY

BOOKS

Anscombe, G. E. M. *Intention.* Oxford, 1957.

Armstrong, D. M. *Belief, Truth, and Knowledge.* Cambridge, 1973.

Chisholm, Roderick M. *Perceiving.* Ithaca, N.Y., 1957.

Dennett, D. C. *Brainstorms.* Montgomery, 1978.

Fodor, J. A. *The Language of Thought.* New York, 1975.

Loar, B. *Mind and Meaning.* Cambridge, 1981.

Woodfield, A., ed. *Thought and Object, Essays on Intentionality.* London, 1982.

ARTICLES

Chisholm, R. M., and W. S. Sellars. "Appendix: Intentionality and the Mental," in *Concepts, Theories, and the Mind-Body Problem,* eds. Feigl, Scriven, and Maxwell, Minnesota Studies in the Philosophy of Science, vol. 2.

Dennett, D., "Making Sense of Ourselves," *Phil. Topics* 12 (1981) 63–81.

———, "Three Kinds of Intentional Psychology," in *Reduction, Time, and Reality,* ed. R. A. Healey, Cambridge, 1981.

———, "Why You Can't Make a Computer That Feels Pain," *Synthese* 38 (1978) 415–456.

Fodor, J. A., "Propositional Attitudes," *Monist* 61 (1978) 501–523.

Locke, Don, "Intention and Intentional Action" in *The Business of Reason,* eds. J. J. MacIntosh and S. C. Coval, London, 1969.

O'Connor, D. J. "Tests for Intentionality," *APQ* 4 (1967) 173–178.

Richardson, R. C., "Internal Representation: Prologue to a Theory of Intentionality," *Phil. Topics* 12 (1981) 171–212.

Sellars, W. S., "Empiricism and the Philosophy of Mind," in his *Science, Perception and Reality,* London, 1963, and in *Foundations of Science and the Concepts of Psychology and Psychoanalysis,* eds. Feigl and Scriven, Minnesota Studies in the Philosophy of Science, vol. 1.

Stich, S., "Dennett on Intentional Systems," *Phil. Topics* 12 (1981) 39–62.

———, "Do Animals Have Beliefs?" *AJP* 57 (1979) 15–28.

———, "On the Ascription of Content," in *Thought and Object, Essays on Intentionality,* ed. A. Woodfield, London, 1982.

van Gulick, R., "Functionalism, Information, and Content," *Nature and System* 2 (1980) 139–162.

PANPSYCHISM

Clifford, W. K. *Lectures and Essays,* vol. 2. London, 1879.

Fechner, G. T. *Religion of a Scientist,* ed. and tr. Walter Lowrie. New York, 1946.

Montague, W. Pepperell, "The Human Soul and the Cosmic Mind," *Mind* 54 (1945) 50–64.

Sellars, R. W., "Panpsychism or Evolutionary Materialism," *Philosophy of Science* 27 (1960) 329–350.

Strong, C. A. *Why the Mind Has a Body.* New York, 1903.

PARAPSYCHOLOGY

Beloff, J. *Psychological Sciences.* London, 1973.

Broad, C. D. *Lectures on Psychical Research.* London, 1962.

————, "The Relevance of Psychical Research to Philosophy," in his *Religion, Philosophy, and Psychical Research,* London, 1953.

Godbey, Jr., J. W., "Central State Materialism and Parapsychology," *Analysis* 36 (1975) 22–25.

Hansel, C. E. M. *ESP: A Scientific Evaluation.* New York, 1966.

Price, Harry. *Fifty Years of Psychical Research.* London, 1939.

Soal, S. G., and Frederick Bateman. *Modern Experiments in Telepathy.* London, 1954.

Vasiliev, L. L. *Experiments in Mental Suggestion.* London, 1963.

QUESTIONS RELATING TO THE MIND-BODY PROBLEM—BUT NOT ADDRESSED TO PARTICULAR VIEWS OF THAT PROBLEM

BOOKS

Chomsky, Noam. *Language and Mind.* New York, 1968.

Geach, Peter. *Mental Acts.* London, 1960.

Hampshire, Stuart. *Thought and Action.* New ed. Notre Dame, 1983.

Harris, E. E. *Nature, Mind and Modern Science.* London, 1954.

James, William. *Principles of Psychology.* New York, 1890.

Kenny, Anthony. *Action, Emotion and Will.* London, 1963.

Russell, Bertrand. *The Analysis of Mind.* New York, 1921.

————, *My Philosophical Development.* London, 1959.

Shoemaker, Sydney. *Self-Knowledge and Self-Identity.* Ithaca, N.Y., 1963.

Shwayder, D. S. *The Stratification of Behavior.* New York, 1965.

Taylor, Charles. *The Explanation of Behavior.* London, 1964.

Taylor, Richard. *Action and Purpose.* Englewood Cliffs, N.J., 1966.

Whiteley, C. H. *An Introduction to Metaphysics.* London, 1950.

ARTICLES

Baier, Kurt, "The Place of a Pain," *Phil. Quarterly* 14 (1964) 138–150.

Brown, Robert, "Moods and Motives," *AJP* 43 (1965) 277–294.

Coburn, Robert C., "Pains and Space," *J. Phil* 63 (1966) 381–396.

Cohen, Mendel F., "Motives, Causal Necessity and Moral Accountability," *AJP* 42 (1964) 322–334.

Cornman, James W., "Private Languages and Private Entities," *AJP* 46 (1968) 117–126.

Davidson, Donald, "Actions, Reasons and Causes," in *Free Will and Determinism,* ed. Bernard Berofsky, New York, 1966.

Lycos, Kim, "Images and the Imaginary," *AJP* 43 (1965) 321–338.

McLaughlin, R. N., "Human Action," *AJP* 45 (1967) 141–158.

Margolis, Joseph, "After-Images and Pains," *Philosophy* 41 (1966) 333–340.

O'Neil, W. M., "Purposivism," *AJP* 25 (1947) 152–173.

Richman, Robert J., "Reasons and Causes: Some Puzzles," *AJP* 47 (1969) 42–50.

Rolston, Howard L., "Kinaesthetic Sensations Revisited," *J. Phil* 62 (1965) 96–100.

Taylor, D. M., "The Location of Pain," *Phil. Quarterly* 15 (1965) 53–62.

Walker, Jeremy, "Embodiment and Self-Knowledge," *Dialogue* 8 (1969) 44–67.

Ziff, Paul, "The Simplicity of Other Minds," *J. Phil* 64 (1965) 575–589.

COLLECTIONS OF ARTICLES

Anderson, A. R., *Minds and Machines*. Englewood Cliffs, N. J., 1964.

Block, N. J., ed. *Readings in the Philosophy of Psychology*, 2 vols. Harvard, 1979.

Borst, C. V., ed. *The Mind-Brain Identity Theory*. London, 1970.

Castañeda, Héctor-Neri, ed. *Intentionality, Minds, and Perception*. Detroit, 1966.

Chappell, V. C., ed. *The Philosophy of Mind*. Englewood Cliffs, N. J., 1962.

Dennett and Hofstatder, eds. *The Minds I*. New York, 1981.

Feyerabend, P. K., and G. E. Maxwell, eds. *Mind, Matter, and Method*. Minneapolis, 1966.

Flew, A. G. N., ed. *Body, Mind, and Death*. New York, 1964.

Gustafson, Donald F., ed. *Essays in Philosophical Psychology*. Garden City, N.Y., 1964.

Guttenplan, S., ed. *Mind and Language*. Oxford, 1975.

Hampshire, Stuart, ed. *Philosophy of Mind*. New York, 1966.

Hook, Sidney, ed. *Dimensions of Mind*. New York, 1961.

O'Connor, John, ed. *Modern Materialism: Readings on Mind-Body Identity*. New York, 1969.

Ross, S. A., and P. A. Roth, eds., "Matters of the Mind," *Synthese* 53 (1982) 157–356.

Scher, J. M., ed. *Theories of the Mind*. New York, 1962.

Shahan, R., ed. *Philosophical Topics* 12 (1981) 9–226.

Smythies, J. R., ed. *Brain and Mind*. London, 1965.

Vesey, G. N. A., ed. *Body and Mind: Readings in Philosophy*. London, 1964.

Wann, T. W., ed. *Behaviorism and Phenomenology*. Chicago, 1964.

INDEX